Internal Control
of Fixed Assets

Internal Control of Fixed Assets

A Controller and Auditor's Guide

ALFRED M. KING

WILEY

John Wiley & Sons, Inc.

Library of Congress Cataloging-in-Publication Data

King, Alfred M.
 Internal control of fixed assets: a controller and auditor's guide/Alfred M. King.
  p. cm.—(Wiley corporate F & A; 564)
 Includes index.
 ISBN 978-0-470-53940-8 (book); ISBN 9781118028346 (ebk);
 ISBN 9781118028353 (ebk); ISBN 9781118028360 (ebk)
 1. Capital. 2. Accounting. I. Title.
 HD39.K527 2011
 658.15'2—dc22   2010045645

Printed in the United States of America

10 9 8 7 6 5 4 3 2 1

*Once again, to the most patient person
and my best friend, my wife,
Mary Jane King.*

Contents

Preface

F OR MANY COMPANIES, FIXED assets, sometimes referred to as Property, Plant, and Equipment (PP&E) represent the largest single asset category on the balance sheet. Yet rarely do fixed assets command management time that is proportionate to the magnitude of the investment. Companies may devote significant resources to capital expenditure budgeting and approval, making extremely detailed calculations about proposed capital outlays. But once the project is completed, and in operation, subsequent record keeping and controls are often lax.

Management usually assumes that since fixed assets are "fixed" there should be little trouble monitoring what is going on. Accountants are concerned with calculating annual depreciation charges, for their company's books and taxes. Occasionally, the property record will be the basis of decisions on insurance coverage for the assets. Even less frequently, property tax assessments may be challenged, but this is often the responsibility of the tax department.

So while there are many uses, and many users, of a good property tax accounting system, the one thing that is usually lacking is a reconciliation of the books of account to the assets actually present physically. While every company takes a physical inventory of raw materials, work in process, and finished goods, very few actually take a look at their "fixed" assets and compare what is there with what the property record says is there.

In short, there is a gap here in Internal Control, a gap that goes on year after year. The assumption is often made, "Well our records might not be perfect, but they were good enough to get by our audit last year, nothing has changed, so we should be okay this year." Further, auditors and managements often are more interested in year to year comparisons rather than the value of absolute amounts. So if this year's depreciation expense can be reconciled to last year's depreciation expense, allowing for additions and deletions, everything is assumed to be correct.

Compounding the issue is that while the subject of Internal Control has generated tremendous interest following adoption of Sarbanes-Oxley (SOX), most efforts have been devoted to areas such as revenue recognition and financial instruments. By and large independent auditors review fixed-asset accounting controls, make sure there have been no changes since the previous audit, and wish for the client to take and reconcile a physical inventory. Many management letters from auditors to audit committees and the Chief Financial Officer (CFO) have almost a boilerplate recommendation that such an audit should be undertaken.

Taking, and reconciling, an inventory of PP&E is a major project. Particularly in a period of retrenchment, when the company has to "do more with less," the priority of a physical inventory of PP&E inevitably "slips" until the next year comes around and the process starts again. This state of affairs continues because PP&E is seen as having a lower priority than many other aspects of Internal Control. Items which command the attention of auditors become a priority of the audit committee. In turn, auditors' priorities are set by their perception of what the Public Company Accounting Oversight Board (PCAOB) is focusing on. And, to date, PCAOB has not put emphasis on their reviews on what the audit firms did with client PP&E. As noted, revenue recognition and financial instruments at fair value seem to have a much higher PCAOB priority.

But what if the PCAOB starts to review auditor workpapers dealing with PP&E on a more intensive basis? Most auditors' workpapers would likely come up short. Unfortunately, if the PCAOB was to start putting PP&E on a priority basis, companies would feel intensive pressure from their external auditors.

As will be discussed in this book, developing a sound system of internal control for fixed assets, and cleaning up past errors and omissions, are not trivial efforts. Realistically they really cannot be done in less than one to two years, assuming that all other financial and operating functions of the business must continue to be carried on at current rates. Put another way, *extra* resources will inevitably have to be devoted to fixing existing fixed-asset systems. This will cost time and money, which most management will begrudge—which of course is the reason we are where we are today.

This is the first comprehensive book to focus on Internal Controls for Fixed Assets. It is a step-by-step guide to developing and maintaining a functioning internal control system that will withstand the closest scrutiny from independent public accountants and ultimately the PCAOB.

We recommend strong internal audit involvement in diagnosing the current condition of the present fixed-asset accounting system. Internal audit should also be involved in the development of specific recommendations for the required remedial work. Performing the actual required work should probably be managed by existing accounting and operations staff often with the help of outside consultants. Depending on the speed with which the company wishes to finish the task, some temporary help may be necessary, and use of an outside consultant may be cost effective.

At the time this is written it is not clear whether the United States will or will not have adopted International Financial Reporting Standards (IFRS). Nonetheless, and in order for this to be valuable even to U.S. subsidiaries that do have to report under IFRS, throughout the book similarities and differences between IFRS and Generally Accepted Accounting Principles (GAAP) will be covered. Two major differences are that under IFRS companies are permitted, although not required, to write up certain assets and investment properties. Second, in case an impairment charge has been taken, a subsequent improvement in the value can be booked, thus reversing the prior impairment charge. Neither of these is currently permitted under GAAP.

As the Financial Accounting Standards Board (FASB) increases the use of fair value, it is possible that PP&E at some time may have to be written up in the United States to current fair value. We briefly touch on this topic, although other books cover this specific subject of fair value in much greater detail. We do cover in detail present requirements for testing for impairment, because this is a subject which potentially affects almost every company.

The primary focus of this book is PP&E, but we also cover briefly certain aspects of intangible assets, primarily those that arise in a business combination.

Because of the importance of SOX compliance, we focus on the role of internal auditing in making sure that companies come as close as possible to full compliance. If independent accountants, given a push from the PCAOB, start to focus on internal controls dealing with PP&E, it will be critical for internal audit staffs to become intimately involved. While the primary emphasis is on the accounting and management control aspects, it is clear that internal audit must be fully knowledgeable of what the current state of affairs is, and what the ultimate goal should be.

Inasmuch as this is probably one of the first books written on the subject, the author will welcome comments and suggestions from readers for subsequent editions (aking@marshall-stevens.com). It is impossible to cover everything of importance and undoubtedly certain topics will have been inadvertently left out. All help will be graciously accepted.

Readers are not expected to sit down and read this book from cover to cover. Rather it should be considered an overall guide to the total subject. Each chapter more or less stands on its own. References to material in other chapters are given. Nonetheless, there is some overlap, and this represents a conscious decision to make the book as user friendly as possible.

Alfred M. King
April 2011

CHAPTER ONE

Internal Control, Sarbanes-Oxley, and the Public Company Accounting Oversight Board

A S WILL BE DISCUSSED in this chapter, most company Chief Executive Officers (CEOs) and Chief Financial Officers (CFOs) are signing an annual certification with the Securities and Exchange Commission (SEC). The certification states that they are complying with the applicable requirements of the Sarbanes-Oxley Act (SOX). What may not be known is that those requirements actually include a mandatory physical inventory of Property, Plant, and Equipment (PP&E) *and* a reconciliation of that inventory to the books of account, with any changes having to be recorded properly.

 ## INTERNAL CONTROLS OVER PROPERTY, PLANT, AND EQUIPMENT–MANDATORY BUT WEAK

It is a rare company indeed that has recently taken a physical inventory of its PP&E, reconciled that inventory to the books of account, and then adjusted the books for ghost[1] and zombie assets. Unless this task is completed, it is hard to see how a CEO and CFO can honestly sign the required SOX certification. A real-life CEO certification in a Form 10-K sent to the SEC goes something like this:

"SECTION 906 OF THE SARBANES-OXLEY ACT OF 2002

In connection with the Annual Report of ___ Inc. (the "Company") on Form 10-K for the period ending September 27, 20xx, as filed with the Securities and Exchange Commission on the date hereof (the "Report"), I, ___, as the Chief Executive Officer of the Company, certify, pursuant to 18 U.S.C. 1350, as adopted pursuant to section 906 of the Sarbanes-Oxley Act of 2002, that, to the best of my knowledge:

(1) The Report fully complies with the requirements of section 13 (a) or 15(d) of the Securities Exchange Act of 1934

(2) The information contained in the Report fairly presents, in all material respects, the financial condition and result of operations of the "Company"

In turn, this requirement in 18 U.S.C. (United States Code) 1350 reads:

"Sec. 1350. Failure of corporate officers to certify financial reports

(a) CERTIFICATION OF PERIODIC FINANCIAL REPORTS–Each periodic report containing financial statements filed by an issuer with the Securities Exchange Commission pursuant to section 13 (a) or 15(d) of the Securities Exchange Act of 1934 (15 U.S.C. 78m(a) or 78o(d)) shall be accompanied by a written statement by the chief executive officer and chief financial officer (or equivalent thereof) of the issuer.

(b) CONTENT–The statement required under subsection (a) shall certify that the periodic report containing the financial statements fully complies with the requirements of section 13(a) or 15(d) of the Securities Exchange Act of 1934 (15 U.S.C 78m(a) or 78o(d)) and that information contained in the periodic report fairly presents, in all material respects, the financial condition and results of operations of the issuer."

The applicable law referenced above reads:

(a) Reports by issuer of security; contents:

(1) Every issuer of a security registered pursuant to section 78l of this title shall file with the Commission, . . .

(2) Such annual reports (and such copies thereof), certified if required by the rules and regulations of the Commission by independent public accountants, . . .

(b) Form of report; books, records, and internal accounting; directives . . .

(2) Every issuer which has a class of securities registered pursuant to section 78l of this title and every issuer which is required to file reports pursuant to section 78o(d) of this title shall—

(A) Make and keep books, records, and accounts, which, in reasonable detail, accurately and fairly reflect the transactions and dispositions of the assets of the issuer

(B) Devise and maintain a system of internal accounting controls sufficient to provide reasonable assurances that—

(i) Transactions are executed in accordance with management's general or specific authorization

(ii) Transactions are recorded as necessary

(I) To permit preparation of financial statements in conformity with generally accepted accounting principles or any other criteria applicable to such statements

(II) To maintain accountability for assets

(iii) Access to assets is permitted only in accordance with management's general or specific authorization

(iv) The recorded accountability for assets is compared with the existing assets at reasonable intervals and appropriate action is taken with respect to any differences

Cutting through all the legalese, these laws and regulations, certified by the CEO and CFO of every publicly traded company, appear to require just what we are writing about in this book. Companies must take a periodic physical inventory of PP&E and then have a reconciliation of that inventory to the books of account. Yet very few companies are actually doing this.

Virtually every company that owns fixed assets, sometimes referred to as Property, Plant, and Equipment, does have a computerized property record system. There are a number of such fixed-asset or property record software systems on the market and most of them do a reasonable job of (1) recording newly acquired assets, (2) computing depreciation expense for books and taxes, and (3) allowing for additions and deletions over time.

The programs have provision for adjustments based on physical inventories, but such capabilities are rarely used. Our professional experience when we actually try and locate assets from the property record system is that up to 15% of the assets cannot be located! Offsetting these "ghost assets" are what we refer to as "zombie assets," which are physically present but not on the property record system.

It would be hard to argue that a record, which is 15% off from economic reality represents internal control that complies with the SOX requirements stated above.

But it is not all bad news. Once a company gets into compliance with an accurate record, one that can and will be maintained properly in the future, there are a number of benefits.

As will be discussed in this chapter and throughout the book, a typical property record system probably meets the needs of the accounting department, which is the requirement for periodic calculation of depreciation expense. Most companies however, at least in the author's experience, do not fully use their property records for many of the following *additional* tasks:

- Internal Control
- Internal Audit of Capital Expenditures
- Maintenance and Condition
- Insurance
- Property Tax
- Return on Investment
- Transfers between departments and plants

Further, while the accounting department is usually the custodian of the records, as well as the principal user, many other departments can and should be involved, as shown in the previous listing. The previous listing is not in random order, and the very first item, internal control, is of critical concern for all publicly traded companies and any privately held firm that could be sold to a public firm at some point in the future.

What is internal control over fixed assets? Internal control means far more than just having a printout of assets that you bought and have not yet fully depreciated. Internal control really means having assurance that the assets you think you own are still there, and that they have not gone missing. While it may not immediately come to mind, internal control also means that you do not have assets physically present that are not on your books at all or zombie assets.

Any generalization that companies are not in compliance with the books and records requirements of the Securities and Exchange Commission (SEC), can be disproved for any single company; it must be admitted that certain firms, particularly in the utility and defense industries, do a pretty good job of internal control. But by and large it is a very safe generalization that most companies have poor, or even nonexistent, controls over PP&E.

Before looking at internal controls over PP&E, let us take a look at an area where virtually all companies do have good internal control systems, that is, working capital.

INTERNAL CONTROLS OVER WORKING CAPITAL

Companies every year send out confirmations to their customers, asking them to verify that the receivables on the books of account represent real liabilities by the customer to the company. Auditors usually carry out this confirmation project, and attempt to reconcile any differences which are uncovered. Certainly when a customer is willing to acknowledge that it owes money this is an indication that the company's control over receivables complies with all applicable internal control requirements.

Any differences in receivables reported by customers or clients then become the basis for further analysis. The reasons that companies do not pay, or withhold payment from their suppliers, are as varied as the human imagination can develop. These excuses for nonpayment are an integral part of the business model of suppliers to retail firms. Yet nonpayment does not indicate a lack of control. It does suggest that there are some problems between the two firms that must be resolved. This is not a responsibility of the auditor, but rather between marketing and production relative to what the customers received, as contrasted to what they thought they would receive. Only on the rare occasion where there is actual fraud do receivables appear to be out of control.

Internal control over inventories is somewhat more difficult, at least in terms of pricing out the items, and assessing whether some of the items on hand are surplus or obsolete. Nonetheless, companies either have a perpetual inventory system that is constantly being tested for accuracy, or they take an annual physical inventory. After pricing out the items on hand, and comparing the total to the book balances, inventory "shrinkage" charges often must be made. Retailers usually budget for such losses, while other manufacturing and wholesale companies attempt to keep writedowns to an absolute minimum. The reason is clear: Adjustments directly hit the profit and loss (P&L) accounts, and reported earnings are going to be reduced.

Pricing out an inventory, depending on the type of company, may involve significant judgment. It is the application of this judgment that auditors review, after assuring themselves that the reported physical quantities are accurate. Two examples of the type of judgment that is required are (1) if the company is on LIFO (last in, first out) and (2) if the merchandise is seasonal and may be unsalable at list price. Valuing inventory is an integral responsibility of every company and it is safe to say that the job is either done properly, or the firm itself is going to be in financial difficulty.

Thus when signing an SOX certification there is little downside risk for the CEO and CFO with respect to working capital. The SOX requirements for internal control obviously go way beyond working capital, particularly for valuing financial instruments and for developing accurate revenue recognition. Such functions are outside the scope of this book. We do cover working capital because all the issues in valuing receivables and inventory are involved in PP&E, as will be discussed in this book.

SECURITIES AND EXCHANGE COMMISSION AND PUBLIC COMPANY ACCOUNTING OVERSIGHT BOARD SCRUTINY OF FINANCIAL STATEMENTS

Similarly, we do not devote effort here to the valuation problems of intangible assets and the determination of whether any of them are impaired or not. Valuation of intangibles is high on the audit requirements of most auditing firms, because of Public Company Accounting Oversight Board (PCAOB) scrutiny; consequently this scrutiny drives management effort. If management did not review intangibles at least once a year, there would be a real threat that the auditing firm could not and would not issue its opinion. Since every company filing with the SEC has to have an auditor's attestation, what gets scrutinized by regulators gets done.

The PCAOB's review of auditing workpapers drives auditing firms to be responsive to what the PCAOB review team checks in their annual review. Knowing the PCAOB will be looking at financial instrument valuation, and revenue recognition puts these functions near the top of an auditor's "to-do" list in the annual audit. Knowing that auditors are going to review financial instruments and intangibles, as well as revenue recognition, means in turn that a company's financial management devotes resources to these tasks. Thus, the signing of the SOX certification for these aspects of internal control does not cause any sleepless nights for CEOs and CFOs.

When it comes to scrutiny over fixed assets, however, the PCAOB so far has not had this very high on its list of things to review in auditor work papers. If the PCAOB is not worrying about something, then with limited time and fee, most auditors will not devote undue resources to client controls over PP&E. If the auditors are not looking at something then company management tends to put any such effort at a very low level.

In short, what gets measured gets done.

WHY DO AUDITORS NOT SPEND MORE TIME ON PROPERTY, PLANT, AND EQUIPMENT?

The standard audit certificate states:

> "In our opinion, the financial statements present fairly, in all material respects, the consolidated financial position of ___ and the consolidated results of operations and its cash flows, in conformity with U.S. generally accepted accounting principles."

Now, generally accepted accounting principles (GAAP) do not deal directly with internal control. The auditor's review of a client's internal control may be performed in conjunction with the financial statement audit, but is actually a quite separate review.

What auditors look for in reviewing annual financial statements of a client involves an understanding of what is going on in the business. Are there any unusual occurrences this year that might mean the client's accounting could be off? Auditors look at this year's P&L and balance sheet, and compare them with the corresponding statements of the prior year and the current year's budget. As long as there is a consistent pattern, the "no news is good news" thought governs their actions.

Now, let us look at the property record system. When a new asset is listed, at a minimum the information recorded is the cost, the salvage value if any, the depreciation method (straight line, declining balance, etc.), and the expected life. From that point on the computer will calculate depreciation expense every month (or every quarter) until the original cost has been written down to zero or to the estimated salvage value.

The calculation of depreciation expense can, and will, go on irrespective of whether or not the asset is actually on hand. Suppose the asset is traded five years later, and the original life estimate was 12 years. If not written off at that time, then for the following seven years the company would continue to record depreciation expense until a zero balance was obtained.

Any audit tests comparing this year's results with last year's, or this year's results with the budget will show a 100% correlation. Even if both years and the budget are wrong, the inexorable march until the asset is fully depreciated will continue. The error, which will never be caught absent a physical inventory, is that the asset is not in use, and should not be recorded as an asset belonging to the company. But on a *comparative* basis, year to year, there is nothing to call attention to this disparity.

There is no reason for the CEO and CFO to worry when they sign the annual statement indicating that there is good internal control. Ignorance is bliss. They truly believe there is no problem and their auditing firm is not telling them anything different. But, and this is a big but, if the company did take an inventory of PP&E, and reconcile it to the books, the missing asset(s) would show up, and a one-time charge would have to be made. Nobody likes sudden write-offs, and if there is no inventory taken there will never be a write-off. Yet, the legal requirements for reconciliation of assets to the books of account do not exempt PP&E. The fact that such work is not performed is understandable but not in accordance with the actual requirements.

As indicated previously, when our firm does actually take a physical inventory of PP&E, usually there will be up to 15% of the assets, which cannot be located. As will be discussed in Chapters 5 and 6, it is almost impossible to avoid having serious errors in the property record unless company management makes this a priority and devotes sufficient resources to maintain an accurate record.

Auditors do not require physical inventories of PP&E because, with limited resources, other aspects of internal control appear to have a higher priority. Annual depreciation expense charges will, eventually, resolve all errors in the system. Meanwhile there is no *apparent* error in reported depreciation expense that would signal the existence of a problem.

What would happen if the PCAOB started reviewing the workpapers of auditors with respect to internal control of the clients' PP&E? Obviously there would be a lot of embarrassment, both at the audit firms and at the companies. There would be a great rush to straighten things out, but as will be discussed in subsequent chapters, taking a physical inventory and reconciling it is a major undertaking, requiring substantial resources and an elapsed time frame. Solving previous problems in the PP&E area is not going to be cheap or quick.

We provide guidance in this book to minimize the effort in taking the inventory, and keeping the cost to a minimum. The one statement that will be true, however, is that the longer this is postponed the greater the time and cost of resolving prior errors. Do not be mistaken. The property records of virtually every company do *not* correspond to physical reality. We discuss in subsequent chapters why this happens, and how to minimize future problems. But there should be no misunderstanding; the initial effort is going to be far from trivial and significant write-offs may be incurred.

 ## WHO IS RESPONSIBLE FOR INTERNAL CONTROL OVER PROPERTY, PLANT, AND EQUIPMENT?

This is a serious question, and one that probably cannot be answered accurately or quickly in most companies.

The initial response will usually be, "Well the accounting department is responsible. They maintain the records, calculate depreciation expense, and record all additions and reductions. Now that we think of it, it really is an accounting department responsibility."

This glib statement, pinning responsibility on accountants, is far from the whole story in terms of true internal control over PP&E. What about operating managers who are responsible for the assets assigned to them? What about the property tax department which prepares schedules submitted to local tax assessors? What about the insurance department responsible for making sure insurance coverage is neither too high, nor too low? If an internal audit department undertook an audit of the company's fixed-asset system, and found serious weaknesses in internal control, who would be responsible for fixing them? Where is the plant engineering and maintenance department that should be able to determine whether it is worthwhile repairing an asset, or scrapping it and replacing it with a new acquisition? The same holds true for companies with serious investment in real estate, with leasehold improvements being a substantial component of overall rental expense.

At this point, having pointed out all the areas of a company, there really is only one answer to the question in the heading as to who is responsible. The true answer has to be senior management. But because the absence of good internal control does not show up immediately, in effect PP&E is an "out of sight, out of mind" issue. Things will continue to go downhill until management becomes convinced that this is a corporate issue, sets forth individual responsibilities, and then provides sufficient resources to maintain the overall system.

Meanwhile the tax department, the insurance department, and the real estate department, as well as engineering, will all be complaining about the accuracy of the records, but will not feel an individual responsibility to "do something" about it. Operating managers, say in a manufacturing environment, worry about meeting production schedules and if they have to cannibalize an existing machine to provide spare parts for another critical piece of equipment, it will be done irrespective of any company policies relating to PP&E. Short-term solutions to apparent short-term problems continue to result in longer-term issues that may not have current visibility but nonetheless are real.

While the property record system is usually in the hands of a company's accounting department, it is totally unrealistic to expect accountants to "control" PP&E. A typical pattern for asset acquisition and disposal might run as follows:

- A department head identifies a prospective capital addition that will either reduce operating and production costs, or increase capacity.
- Financial analysts "scrub" the proposal, and if the analysis is favorable a higher level executive approves the project; depending on the size some projects have to go as high as the Board of Directors.
- Purchasing and engineering, depending on the project, design and order the equipment.
- A construction-in-progress (CIP) account may be set up to accumulate the costs.
- The final payments are made, including freight and installation and debugging, and the appropriate amount is transferred from CIP to fixed assets.
- The tax department determines the appropriate tax treatment while the controller's department determines the appropriate life, salvage value if any, and accounting life.
- Any trade-in of old equipment is removed from the existing property record, and a gain or loss could be recognized.
- In many firms the maintenance or plant engineering department will tie in maintenance records and information into the overall property record system.
- If the asset is moved from one operating department to another, or one plant location to another, the appropriate information is supposed to be transmitted to the accounting department so as to update the record for insurance and property taxes.
- Depending on the company's accounting policy, book depreciation expense will be charged to the department that "owns" the asset.
- Perhaps someone from the internal audit staff will "review" the property accounting system.
- Occasionally, some junior from the outside audit firm will "test" a sample of the entries made that year, to see that the amount capitalized ties out to the vendor invoices.

- At some point in the future the asset will be fully depreciated for books of account and tax purposes, but if it is functioning the asset will remain physically even though no accounting or tax entries are being generated.
- In many firms the current replacement cost is determined through application of appropriate cost indices, and the resulting information used for placement of insurance by the insurance department.
- At some point, either before being fully depreciated, or after all depreciation charges have been taken, the asset will be disposed of and a debit or credit generated.

Why go through what is in many firms a very common series of steps? We hope this demonstrates the significant number of functional organizations involved with the overall fixed-asset process. Expecting some low-level property accountant to keep on top of all this, absent serious management support, is simply unrealistic.

Further, without denigrating the vast majority of property accountants who try very hard, in many business organizations the property tax accounting function is not viewed as a stepping stone to more substantial financial management jobs. All too often the property accountant is either the newest hire in the accounting department, or the job is given to "good old Harry" who will be retiring next year after 33 years of faithful service to the company.

The truth is that property accounting is *not* glamorous. It is hard for a property accountant to demonstrate initiatives that will help the company increase profits. Certainly, financial managers in cost accounting, budgeting, financial analysis, and taxes can feel a real sense of satisfaction at how their work "helps" the company meet its primary objective of producing and selling products and services at a profit. All too often the property accounting function is little more than an afterthought. After all, "we just acquired a fixed-asset software system that does everything we need!" which is often followed by the stated, or unstated, thought "Really, what's so hard about the job?"

 ## "WHAT IS SO HARD ABOUT THE JOB?"

The answer to this question is simple. Review the 15 bullets in the list above. Virtually all of the functions listed have to be performed; if they are not coordinated then it is an absolute certainty that the property record system will not reflect actual assets owned by the company. At that point the certifications by the CEO and CFO simply are incorrect. The fact that neither the PCAOB nor the SEC has so far pursued this aspect of internal control is by no means the same as telling companies: "Don't worry about signing the SOX certification if your internal controls on PP&E do not comply. We will grant you a blanket exemption because the people who wrote the laws and regulations didn't really mean to include the 30 to 40% of your total assets tied up in PP&E."

Getting and maintaining a satisfactory system of Internal Control over PP&E is a difficult job, one that involves many different people in an organization. As will be discussed later, in Chapter 3 some one individual or department has to have the overall responsibility for the system. But the job cannot be done in a vacuum. Senior management, that is those signing the SOX certification, has to provide the resources, and management coordination, that will allow the property accountant to get her/his job done.

A simple review of almost any firm's current balance sheet will show that the original cost of the land, buildings, machinery, and equipment represents a sizable portion of total assets. In many manufacturing firms the PP&E is greater in magnitude than inventory and receivables combined. As discussed before, companies and auditors put a lot of attention on making sure that the books and records for inventory and receivables are accurate. At some point equal attention will be focused on PP&E.

Getting an existing system correct, scrubbing out all the errors that exist, and assuring that future efforts will not lead to a recurrence of today's problem is a major effort, both in time and resources. No one will guarantee that if you have started the recovery project, but not yet finished it, that your company and its management will not be faulted. What is certain is that if you are in the middle of such a recovery project you will be far ahead of those firms who have not yet woken up to the magnitude of their problem.

The remainder of this book will take you through the steps we recommend. Once they are followed, you will have a system that will stand up to the scrutiny of the most hard-nosed auditor, SEC enforcement official, or PCAOB reviewer. It will be a long journey, a hard and expensive journey, but you will arrive at the prize that awaits you at the end of the proverbial rainbow.

 NOTE

1. Ghost assets are items on the books of account that cannot be located. Zombie assets are items that are physically present, but not on the books of account. These will be discussed in detail in subsequent Chapters 7 and 8.

2

Capitalization versus Expense

O NE OF THE MOST important decisions that company management must make deals with the capitalization policy. Specifically, what purchases will be expensed as incurred and what purchases will be capitalized and depreciated over time?

This is not a trivial issue. Simply saying "because we have always done it this way" is *not* a substitute for serious analysis. In some ways the entire process of internal control of fixed assets depends on the initial decision as to when expensing stops and capitalization starts.

The actual range that different companies use is far wider than might be imagined. In today's environment it is unusual to find anyone capitalizing purchases of less than $500 per item, although there are firms with lower levels. Yet a significant number of companies have a policy of capitalizing all fixed assets acquired in excess of $500. At the other extreme, one large construction and engineering firm expenses everything under $25,000.

CAPITALIZATION THEORY

The basic accounting theory supporting the capitalization of long-lived assets, often referred to as Property, Plant, and Equipment (PP&E), is that assets which have a useful life longer than a year should have the initial cost spread over the "useful life." By definition, for long-lived assets the useful life always is longer than a year.

By capitalizing the initial cost, and spreading the depreciation over subsequent years, a company is considered to be "matching" costs and revenues. It just takes a minute to realize if all capital costs were expensed in the year of acquisition, reported net income would be essentially wiped out during years of expansion. Then if a company reached a steady-state, or were even declining, the absence of expense charges for assets used in the business would tend to "overstate" income.

Many readers of this book were taught, in their early accounting classes, the importance of matching income and expense, revenues and costs. That is why we use accrual accounting and not cash-based accounting. For many years accrual accounting, which matches inflows and outflows to measure operating profitability, was the basis of virtually all accounting efforts. And, to a great extent, the system worked reasonably well, with a few anomalies that were usually overlooked.

In the mid-1970s the Financial Accounting Standards Board (FASB) started to review the fundamental concepts of accounting. One of the first results of this review was essentially an abandonment of the matching concepts in favor of what is often called an "asset and liability approach."

The asset and liability approach put primacy on the accuracy of a company's balance sheet, and asserted that, at least in theory, net income for a period was the difference between beginning and ending net assets. So, put another way, net income was the difference between beginning and ending net worth, adjusted for stock sales, redemptions, and dividends.

In turn this balance sheet approach focused attention on how assets and liabilities were valued. Simply carrying over original historical cost, particularly in periods of rapid technological change and/or inflation, was felt to distort the financial statements. It was deemed to be far better to show the *current* fair value of the assets and liabilities as contrasted with the original costs. By doing this, readers of a company's financial statements would have a better idea as to what a company as a whole was "really" worth.

A further advantage of carrying assets and liabilities at fair value would be to preclude potential manipulation by management. Many firms, when under pressure to report higher net income, would carefully sell those assets whose current value was in excess of its original depreciated cost. Such "cherry picking" was both common and criticized by security analysts, journalists, and accounting professors.

Regardless of the theoretical benefit of having companies show all assets and liabilities at fair value, the FASB and Securities and Exchange Commission (SEC) moved very slowly. As this is written only financial instruments, in the broadest sense, are being shown at fair value, while other long-lived assets and intangible assets continue to be shown on the balance sheet at depreciated original cost. However, in a business combination, the buyer must put all acquired assets of the target company on its balance sheet at the fair value current at the date of purchase.

Many financial reporting participants, particularly security analysts and academics, have urged the FASB to require the use of fair value on more assets and liabilities, including self-developed intangibles. The preparer community, company financial officers, has argued strongly for *not* making the change and the FASB has so far listened to such arguments.

If the security analysts and academics have been unsuccessful in persuading the FASB to expand the use of fair value, there has been a parallel push that appears to be gaining traction, that is, a requirement for greater disclosures of cash flows. One of the required statements companies have to prepare every time they publicly release financial information is a Statement of Cash Flows often referred to in the past as a statement on the Sources and Uses of Funds. While somewhat technical in nature, there has been persistent criticism as to how companies prepare and disseminate their cash flow information. Pressure has been building for companies to adopt, in essence, a parallel reporting system of actual direct cash flows based on a three-part breakdown into operations, financing, and investment.

How does this digression into accounting theory tie into PP&E? Very simply. The lower the capitalization level, the more that expenditures for PP&E will show up in the investment category with fewer outlay dollars in the operating segment. Greater attention is paid by analysts to cash flow from operations, so companies have an incentive to maximize reported capital expenditures, minimize reported operating expenses, and maximize reported operating income.

Accountants today still urge clients to match revenues and expenditures. In turn this suggests to companies that the more PP&E expenditures that they capitalize, the higher will be the reported cash flow from operations, offset by higher expenditures for investment. Financial analysts place a premium on maximizing cash flow. Under the matching approach, the fair value approach, and the cash flow approach, auditors continue to urge companies to properly account for capital expenditures. This essentially encourages firms to set, and retain, quite low capitalization thresholds.

To sum up at this point, the lower the capitalization level, the more expenditures will be capitalized and the less they will be reported as operating expenses. Of course, subsequent depreciation expense, on an annual basis, will be higher. But since many analysts disregard depreciation expense, assuming it is a "noncash" charge, companies think they will put themselves in the best possible light by maximizing capitalization.

 ## WHY CAPITALIZATION LEVELS MATTER

Companies have limited resources. Demands for efficiency and productivity continue. This is not to mention trying to beat this year's budget and forecasting even better results for next year. But both human ingenuity, and time available, are limited. At some point managers have to face up to reality.

As a manager, if employment cannot increase, you may have to reduce the workload—some tasks simply may not get done. An excellent place to start is with the resources devoted to the control over fixed assets. Put in fewer resources, and then ask the staff to do less!

There is a direct correlation between the costs of running a fixed-asset system, and the number of assets you are trying to control with that system. Now this correlation is not totally linear (a 15% drop in cost for a 15% reduction in assets would be linear) but most financial managers would agree that total costs will go down *if you control fewer assets*. Similarly, if you *add* assets to the system it is realistic to assume some *increase* in costs. Many controllers, in developing budgets, tend to assume that most selling, general, and administrative (SG&A) costs are fixed during periods of growth and should be variable on the downside. Reality is that costs tend to go up more or less proportionately with volume and are perceived to be fixed in nature only in a downturn.

This discussion on costs leads to our critical point: **"Reduce the costs of internal control by controlling *fewer* assets."**

Then the natural question is *"How* do you control fewer assets?" The simplest, and least controversial, way is to raise the minimum level at which asset acquisitions are capitalized, as opposed to charging them directly to expense. If you raise the minimum capitalization limit from $500 to $1,500, as an example, you might reduce by 15 to 20% the total number of asset lines in the fixed-asset ledger. A further increase, to $3,500, could reduce the number of asset lines by a further 30 to 40%.

There is a very simple way to test this hypothesis in your own company. Sort the existing asset ledger in descending order by original asset cost. Determine how many assets are shown with an *original cost* less than $1,500 and by less than $3,500. Then determine the dollar value of the assets less than $1,500 and less than $3,500. The Pareto principle[1] undoubtedly will hold true and a disproportionately large number of the asset listings will account for a relatively small portion of the overall dollar value. By adopting a $3,500 minimum capitalization level, a company can dramatically reduce its workload in controlling fixed assets.

In Chapters 6 through 8 there is a discussion of the physical control of PP&E, the taking of a physical inventory and reconciliation of that inventory to the current ledger. If you have fewer assets to inventory and reconcile, it obviously will take less time and resources, perhaps by more than 50%.

Another way of looking at this issue of internal control is this. Most companies have not reconciled in a long time what is physically there with what the books of account assume is there. A major reason for postponing such reconciliation is the sheer magnitude of the project. Most companies have literally thousands of line items in their property ledger. Trying to find and then tie out thousands of individual assets is a monumental task, one that is all too easily postponed "until we have time for it." Of course such time never arrives and the reconciliation remains an item on the "to-do" list.

In short, the task of demonstrating that there is in fact good control over fixed assets has to become manageable. It is unmanageable to try and find every desk, chair, and filing cabinet in the office, or every tool and die in a manufacturing plant.

If it is unmanageable to locate and reconcile thousands of smaller assets, then why set them up in the first place? The real issue for most companies is this: "Is it better to control 70 to 80% of my assets, or *not* control 100% of my assets?"

Note that the law and SEC certification requirements do not say anything about minimum capitalization levels. All they require is that you be able to demonstrate that whatever has been capitalized is physically there, or the books themselves have been adjusted. Put a different way, there is nothing in the concept of internal control that mandates a specific minimum capitalization level.

CONSEQUENCES OF INCREASING MINIMUM CAPITALIZATION LEVEL

There appear to be three primary objections raised whenever this approach to raise capitalization levels is presented:

1. There will be problems with the Internal Revenue Service (IRS).
2. In the periods just after the switch, reported expenses will be increased.
3. Company will "lose control" over smaller assets, including technology such as personal computers and cell phones.

Internal Revenue Service Issues of a Higher Capitalization Limit

The IRS essentially wants to preclude companies changing accounting policies simply to have the effect of reducing taxable income.

But what they do not want for companies to do on their own volition, the IRS is more than willing to do if it will raise revenue. Look at the current inventory capitalization rules. A number of years ago the IRS required companies to capitalize more overhead expenses in calculating the "cost" of inventory.

An increase in the overhead being capitalized is equivalent to reducing current period operating expenses and increasing taxable income. Any such change, however, works for only a period of a few years. Let us say that inventory turns over once a year, at least for this discussion. If companies have $10 million of sales and $6 million of inventory, then there will also be direct production costs for goods sold of that $6 million, and gross profit is obviously $4 million. If total SG&A expenses were $2.5 million then taxable income for the year would be reported at $1.5 million.

But if the IRS said you had to put $500,000 of your SG&A into inventory (reducing SG&A to $2 million) then at the end of the year you would have $6.5 million carrying value (physical quantities are being held constant) and $2 million of taxable income.

But look at the second year. Now you have the same $10 million of sales; $6.5 million comes out of inventory into cost of goods sold so gross profit is $3.5 million. Subtracting the now current $2 million of SG&A leaves you with $1.5 million of taxable income, the exact same amount as before the required capitalization.

What this means is that changing an amount from expense to capitalization in a particular year has only a one-time impact; after that everything reverts to the same as with the prior accounting. By changing the inventory capitalization rules, the IRS forced companies to show a one-time increase in taxable income in the year of change. This change also had the effect of considerably increasing the cost of maintaining the new accounting–the rules as to just what expenses should and should not be capitalized were often not as clear as they could have been. The accounting work went up forever, and the government received only a small one-year boost in the corporate income taxes it collected.

Now the same principle applies to the concepts enunciated here, where we recommend that companies increase the minimum capitalization level. This will have the impact of increasing expense in the year of change, reducing taxable income for a brief period. But over a three or four year period the impact zeroes out as future depreciation is reduced as a consequence of fewer assets being capitalized. This makes the reasonable assumption that low-cost items previously capitalized also had short lives. If, to the contrary, a company has a sizable file of low-cost items on its property record with long lives, the sheer increase in accounting cost over that time period has to be considered as truly non-value-added work for the accounting staff and the tax department.

It is hard to come up with a single rule of thumb that says changing minimum capitalization will balance out in a specific number of years. You can make a rough calculation by looking to see what total depreciation expense is as a percentage of depreciable assets. If assets turn over in eight years, then at the end of the fourth year the financial impact of any change will pretty much be absorbed, particularly if the company is not making significant annual increases in capital expenditures (capex).

We know of no firm that has explicitly asked the IRS for "permission" to change its capitalization level, although certainly in history there has to have been at least one firm. What the IRS response might have been, or actually was, is not known to this author. Common sense, however, suggests that a gradual increase over a period of years should not have a major impact on overall taxable income.

So if a company currently has a $500 capitalization level and wants to go to $2,500, it might be advisable to increase the dollar amount $500 per year for four years. It should be remembered that IRS audits of many corporate income tax returns are done only once every few years, with the revenue agent looking at two, three, or even four years in one examination.

As stated, any change in accounting of say $500 a year is going to be pretty small initially (how many items are being bought between $501 and

$999 each year?) and then the offset of future lower depreciation expense will start kicking in.

There is a further argument in favor of this approach. A change from a $500 level to a $2,500 level, carried out over a four to five year period, essentially will reflect only the impact of offsetting the inflation that has actually occurred over the past 15, 20, or 25 years. Look at it this way, if $500 was correct 25 years ago then $2,500 today has the same financial impact in relation to prices paid for capex items.

This is similar to LIFO (last in, first out) where higher and higher current costs go into cost of sales each year reducing the dollar amount of inventory on the books of accounts. In subsequent chapters we discuss adjusting asset costs for inflation in response to insurance requirements, which should be on the basis of current replacement costs, not original costs. So there are really two reasons, which can explain for tax purposes what is proposed here. You are offsetting inflation, and the net difference is a one-time only reduction in income or a decrease in taxes paid.

Finally, in this discussion of taxes let us look briefly at property taxes. Most tax jurisdictions rely initially on self-reporting by the taxpayer of new capital additions. While technically a company probably could report differently to the local assessor amounts that differ from internal accounting records, it is our observation that simply to simplify the reporting process virtually all firms use the same amounts.

Thus, by increasing the capitalization limit and reducing the dollars reported each year to the local assessors, ultimately there should be a small, yet meaningful, reduction in property taxes paid.

Reported Expense Will Increase as Capitalization Limit Goes Up

The second argument against changing capitalization limits is the mirror image of what was just discussed for taxes. Yes, reported expense will go up in the year(s) of change. Depreciation will continue to be recorded on previously capitalized small-dollar value assets, and current purchases of small-dollar assets will now be expensed.

Consequently, there is no way around this. Changing capitalization levels will have a small but positive impact on taxes and an offsetting negative impact on reported income.

How often does a company make an investment with short-term negative consequences in order to obtain a greater long-term gain? This is not the place to argue about an over-emphasis on short-term earnings. Those who "pooh-pooh" the importance of earnings have never been responsible to shareholders and security analysts. Having said that, management is paid to make that kind of decision, trading off near-term pain for long-term gain.

There is no doubt that better internal control can be obtained if limited resources are not spread so widely that nothing ever is completed. The basic principle has to be: **"It is better to really control 80% of your PP&E than to pretend that you are controlling 100% of PP&E, while failing at it."**

If in order to accomplish this goal you have to take a short-term "hit" to reported earnings (in fact a favorable impact on cash flow because of tax savings), that is the kind of judgment that CFOs (Chief Financial Officers) are paid to make.

Raising Capitalization Limits Loses Control over Some Assets

This critique totally misses the point. There is no necessary connection between capitalization of assets and actual physical control over those assets. There is nothing in generally accepted accounting principles (GAAP) or Sarbanes-Oxley (SOX) that says there is only one way to keep track of assets. Internal control implies three quite separate and distinct things:

1. Assets are on the books and recorded properly.
2. Assets are physically present.
3. The current value of assets is not less than the book value (i.e., there is no impairment).

Obviously if items are charged to expense when acquired, there is no issue of possible impairment. However, it is totally feasible to have a record of assets that were purchased, and for which physical presence is important, without having them show up as an asset in the property ledger. As an example, take personal computers, which is the asset most frequently brought up in these discussions.

There are software systems that will record each personal computer the company owns, what software, and what versions of that software the user has access to. One can keep track of operating problems, parts replacement, expected life, and so forth in a separate file. The point is that one can maintain control over assets, without capitalizing them for the balance sheet.

Put a different way, a company should not give up control over IT assets, even items as small as a Blackberry. But if the individual items are under the minimum capitalization level, and hence charged to expense when acquired, it is still possible to assign responsibility to those entrusted with the assets.

If this approach is followed then a company's IT department can and should have the overall authority for IT assets. Company policies can be set up, enforced, and monitored for all IT assets. It is just that in terms of internal control, for SOX compliance, there will be many fewer assets that a company has to reconcile to its books of account.

As discussed in subsequent chapters, it is imperative that companies have a regular policy, one that is adhered to and enforced, verifying that assets are where they are supposed to be and reconciling any differences. For IT assets already charged to expense when bought, one can verify that they are actively being used by the employee(s) to whom they were assigned. But if, for example, a terminated employee "walks off" with a $700 computer, this will not show up as a reconciling item on the profit and loss (P&L) statement. If that did happen frequently it might suggest better coordination between Human Resources and IT, but in terms of the formal internal control system mandated by SOX, for which the CEO (Chief Executive Officer) and CFO have to sign annually, keeping track of low-dollar amount IT assets is not required.

 ## WHAT IS THE OPTIMUM CAPITALIZATION LIMIT?

When we have taken surveys of company policies, it appears that some public firms still use $500, and many companies use $1,000, as their capitalization cut-off. Dollar amounts for internal policies range upward, and the occasional large fixed-asset intensive firms can have a $25,000 cutoff. In exceptional circumstances such a high level probably makes sense, but in today's business environment a maximum $5,000 cut-off would appear appropriate.

Now, as discussed previously, if a company currently has a $500 limit, it would probably be unwise suddenly to increase this tenfold. A $500 or $1,000 increase per year, until the $5,000 limit is reached, is supportable as a sound operating policy and will minimize any distortions to P&L and probably obviate any serious IRS concerns.

It should be stated here, at least for the record, that there is no requirement for companies to use the same capitalization limit for financial statements (internal control) and for IRS requirements. Almost all companies do use the same limits, to minimize the work in entering the asset into the property record system.

Virtually all personal computer-based fixed-asset software systems have provisions for different costs or bases for books and for taxes. Many companies use different depreciation methods for books and taxes, so conceptually once you are running two parallel systems it does not add materially to the workload to start with different initial asset costs.

The disadvantage of having separate records and depreciation methods for books and taxes is that when this occurs, GAAP requires deferred tax accounting. There certainly is something positive to say about minimizing or even eliminating such differences. But there is absolutely no requirement in GAAP, or IRS regulations, that the same dollar amount and depreciation methods must be used. It is only in LIFO accounting that there is a mandatory use for financial statements if a company is going to use LIFO for taxes. Fixed-asset accounting can be separate without violating any known requirements.

In fact, some companies will even use different asset cost figures for submission to county tax assessors than they use for internal control purposes and capitalization and a third cost or basis for income taxes. This will be discussed in more detail in Chapter 3; here it only further supports our recommendation that capitalization levels be as high as possible for financial statements and internal control so as to minimize the physical inventory and concurrent reconciliations.

Many company policies and controls date back before the availability of easy-to-use personal computer-based software. Without dating myself, the author saw manual records in many firms, the information kept on separate ledger cards, with depreciation being calculated manually.

Then came mainframe computer software systems. Such systems could be programmed to do anything management could want or imagine. But the programming effort had to be made by the IT department, and in most companies resources never seemed to be available to "tweak" the software. Most companies simply used the existing built-in capabilities of the mainframe software and gave up trying to make it more "user-friendly."

It has only been with the advent of powerful personal computers and specially designed software systems for use on personal computers that companies now have a degree of flexibility they never had before. A good personal computer-based fixed-asset system can do ten times more today than the most advanced mainframe systems could in the 1980s. What has not changed in many companies however is a lack of desire to utilize the full capabilities of today's sophisticated software. Many CFOs and controllers really give very little thought to PP&E, and the lower-level employee tasked with maintaining the records often takes the path of least resistance and that is to continue doing things "the way we always have."

SUMMARY

There is nothing in GAAP or SOX that specifies what a company's minimum capitalization level should be. Limits range, in actual situations, from $500 to $25,000. The higher the limit chosen the fewer will be the assets falling into that category. The fewer the assets in the property ledger, the easier it is to find them and reconcile an actual inventory to the underlying record.

Most companies dread the thought of taking an inventory of their PP&E for two reasons. It is time consuming and expensive, as well as being almost impossible to reconcile to the actual records. If there are major discrepancies, it may be necessary to book an impairment charge. We have yet to meet a CFO or controller who views an impairment charge as any less painful than a root canal. In practice it has been easier to do nothing, than to undertake an inventory that will be costly in several dimensions.

But to the extent that the PCAOB (public company accounting oversight board) and SEC, in the future, start to put pressure on companies and their auditors, to verify and validate internal control over PP&E, it is highly desirable to get "ahead of the curve" before there is too much scrutiny. The first step is to set a reasonable minimum capitalization limit, if necessary, getting to the chosen amount over a period of years.

During the period of change there may be some incremental expense during the years of conversion, and there is always a chance the IRS will come in and object. If companies really are worried about such an occurrence then today's personal computer-based software can easily handle book and tax differences.

NOTE

1. The Pareto principle (also known as the 80-20 rule, the law of the vital few, and the principle of factor sparsity) states that, for many events roughly 80% of the effects come from 20% of the causes. Business management thinker Joseph M. Juran suggested the principle and named it after Italian economist Vilfredo Pareto, who observed that 80% of the land in Italy was owned by 20% of the population.

CHAPTER THREE

Asset Life Cycle—Controls and Software

NASMUCH AS THE TITLE of this book uses the phrase "internal control" this is the place to begin the details. Fundamental to every fixed-asset system is the principle that *all* transactions are properly recorded. You can ask whether this might be considered a tautology. It is self-evident that you cannot control something if you do not know where it is.

The phrase many years ago, "It's 11:00 pm, do you know where your children are?" got to that point very quickly. Unless you know where your children are and what they are doing, bad things *can* happen. Knowing where some asset or person is does not of itself assure good results; similarly not knowing does not mean that bad things are certain to happen. But, as a broad generalization the more knowledge you have, the better off you will be.

The reason for this brief homily is simple. Most companies today have a poor idea both of what assets they own *and* where they are. Fixed-asset records, when we examine them, rarely reflect underlying circumstances.

What usually happens is that *new* acquisitions of fixed assets are properly entered into the fixed-asset system, but that is the end. Where they are today, and what has happened to them since acquisition is usually not clear from the property register.

The fixed-asset software is asked to crank out a report on depreciation expense once a quarter for the period, which is then entered via journal voucher to the trial balance. Companies rely on the depreciation calculation and assume it is totally correct, because "the machine can't make a mistake." If the asset had been set up with a ten-year life and no salvage value, then the dollar amount of monthly, quarterly, or annual depreciation undoubtedly will be correct. This is true irrespective of the depreciation method, accelerated, or straight-line. But an accurate depreciation charge is *not* the same thing as controlling the asset.

Many things can happen to an asset while it is owned. Just a few of the occurrences, which should be reported, but may not have been included, are:

- Loss (employee quits and takes computer).
- Transfer (original department does not have the asset, while the new department pays no attention to what location the property record shows).
- Trade-in (vendor accepts existing asset as a trade-in but company does not remove the old asset from the record).
- Parts salvaged to fix another machine (in manufacturing a good plant engineer will strip parts from an idle machine to keep another unit in production).
- Building addition adds a new wing, but old common wall is not removed from the record when torn down, thus inflating the "value" of the building.
- Fraud (WorldCom staff "created" fictitious assets to inflate reported income).
- Asset shows no book value because it is more than ten years old when a ten-year life had been originally assigned. The fully depreciated asset is removed from the property register, but the asset is still actively in use.
- To avoid capital expenditure limitations major asset is acquired through a series of small invoices, each of which are charged to expense, thus not showing the asset on company records.

In theory, each of these occurrences should have caused information to be given to the accounting department so the property register was updated and accurate. More often than not, however, such notification is *not* made.

There are exceptions to this observation; in some firms, the proper information is made available, recorded, and used. Such instances are few and far between. Utilities and defense contractors, whose income can be a function of the asset base, do a good job. Most other firms treat the property accountant as a second-class citizen and the property record system as a necessary but less important requirement, where the least cost and least effort appears to be justified.

Sometimes if assets are traded in (which by the way is less common than often thought) the accounting department will be notified; an entry will be made deleting the original cost and accumulated depreciation and adjusting the current net book value for a gain or loss. Similarly, when assets are transferred within the business the accounting system is sometimes provided information with which to make the appropriate entry.

All too often, however, the fixed-asset accountant is the last to know of what is transpiring on the shop floor, in the warehouse, or in the administrative offices. Operating managers are under continuous pressure to keep things going and at the same time keep expenses to a minimum. There is more work to do than time available; nonessential tasks are postponed and then forgotten. Unfortunately, notifying the accounting department about changes in fixed assets is perceived by most operating personnel as truly "nonessential."

An objective assessment of the facts stated in the previous paragraph supports this reality. There is no apparent benefit to a particular operating manager in communicating with the accounting department about changes in Property, Plant, and Equipment (PP&E) under his control. Filling out one more "useless" form for accountants to record what happened appears totally unessential. Who is using which assets will never have priority unless and until control over fixed assets becomes a corporate goal—a goal enforced by top management.

This is not the place once again to review the benefits of a good fixed-asset system that provides true internal control. From this point on we assume that company management, as well as operating executives, believe that good internal control is essential and are willing to devote the necessary resources to achieve this objective. The question at this point is, how a company should set up the underlying reporting system in order to control PP&E; the overarching goal should be that internal control costs are minimized and the benefits maximized.

 ## SOFTWARE IS THE KEY

In recent years very powerful software programs have been developed that run on personal computers. Before around 1970 most property records were kept manually on index cards. Then the era of mainframe computers arrived and for the first time companies were readily able to keep both book and tax records for specific assets.

The problem with the mainframe programs was threefold:

1. Each type of mainframe (IBM, Honeywell, Unisys) required a separate version of the software, which meant that providers had difficulty meeting the unique software needs of each potential client.
2. Running output from the programs required scheduling by the information technology department, which effectively meant that immediate access to the records was difficult, including new asset additions and changes.
3. Any changes in accounting requirements or reorganization of a client's business meant major programming was required at a time when programming resources were severely limited.

The advent of powerful PCs in the 1990s provided the basis of a solution to these problems. It is safe to say that today very few companies rely on their property records being on a mainframe system. One exception might be clients of Oracle and SAP, where those providers of enterprise resource planning (ERP) systems try to be "all things to all people." Many users even of those enterprise systems maintain the actual fixed-asset reporting and controls on one of the stand-alone PC systems.

Today on the market there are perhaps a half dozen PC-based fixed asset software systems. We are not in a position to review the pros and cons of each system. At least on the surface most of the systems can perform most required functions, so the final choice of a vendor has to be company specific. For this book we developed working relationships with both Real-Asset Management and Sage. In this chapter we rely on the capabilities (inputs and outputs) of those systems, but this in no way implies that other suppliers cannot provide equivalent capabilities.

The amount of flexibility built into the PC systems is truly remarkable for those who grew up using mainframe systems, where flexibility was definitely lacking. For mainframes, efficient processing trumped user flexibility, so any time a new report was desired programmers had to be involved, including even minor modifications of existing reports.

The one certainty about software and computers is that once information has been captured—and is available—users will come up with unanticipated types of desired reports. Today's software makes this easy.

For companies seriously considering upgrading their internal controls over fixed assets, we strongly recommend acquiring current state-of-the-art PC-based software. The initial cost of the software is extremely low, usually less than $5,000, compared to the multiple benefits which the current products provide. As will be discussed in Chapters 6, 7, and 8, the real cost of upgrading an existing fixed-asset system is in determining just what assets you do have, what you no longer have, and how to reconcile the physical inventory to the existing database. Since this is a major undertaking it makes little sense to try and do it with older and less flexible software.

Buy the best software and at least it will not be a hindrance in any way to the final fully controlled fixed-asset system.

 ## INPUT, OUTPUT, AND REPORTING CAPABILITY

Fixed-asset software has input and output capabilities, in addition to being able to manipulate and calculate all required information. It seems to make sense to evaluate the choice of software by looking first at the *output* reports which the software is capable of producing. Almost by definition, if software is designed to produce a specific printed output, it has to have the capability of having the required data inputted. Thus, output capability should be the deciding criterion in selecting software, assuming price and compatibility with existing records, are more or less equal.

Then look at the input and output requirements, although for most systems there will be relatively little difference. Over any extended period of time, labor costs to maintain the system are going to far outweigh any initial software costs. Consequently, it would pay to test out the competing software products for ease of use and flexibility in processing. If the vendor does not support a specific output requirement, how easy is it to develop it. Can you do it in-house, or do you have to go to the vendor for help?

The software vendors such as Sage and Real Asset provide samples of the most common output forms. Because of the flexibility inherent in PC-based software, if you need a specific output not shown in the standard complement, it will be very easy to provide this. Such potentially unique outputs can probably be prepared by your own staff, and the software firms have full capability to help with almost any conceivable requirement.

With regard to the standardized input forms, the current software has room for a virtually unlimited number of fields. As just a single example, we recommend that in a business combination the acquirer carry over the original asset information from when the item was acquired by the seller. This would be in addition to the new "allocated" purchase price required for the buyer's books, the amount that will be used to calculate future depreciation. Not that you will continue to depreciate the original dollar cost but that you will have that information for subsequent analysis. Future property tax assessments, and insurable values, are often predicated on the original cost of the asset from the original vendor, not the allocated cost arising from the business combination.

HOW TO EVALUATE SOFTWARE VENDORS

The easy way, but the wrong way, to evaluate a prospective acquisition of new PC-based fixed-asset software is to request proposals from the half dozen major suppliers of fixed-asset software, and then select the "low-cost bidder."

The proper way is somewhat more involved, but will arrive at a far superior solution. The first step for the CFO (chief financial officer) and controller to decide is whether the accounting function should lead the analysis, or whether this is an "Information Technology" responsibility. Recommendation: Have the manager to whom the property accountant reports be in charge of the selection process, with advice from IT and the property accountant. If internal control is the goal, and it should be, then leaving decisions to the technical analysis of a software analyst will totally miss the point. As a generalization, IT folk like efficiency, whereas the goal in fixed assets is to get maximum control with the least management time and effort.

We suggest then that you contact probably three, but no more than four, vendors and ask them to visit you. This way the representative will obtain an understanding of what you are currently doing, will explain the capabilities of his particular suite of programs, and can then make recommendations.

It is important that you ask for a specific proposal, focused on your company's needs. Undoubtedly, the software firm will have gone through this before and should be able to make some pretty specific suggestions. Ask them for the unique aspects of their system, and how such capabilities can help you.

Then if you have three or four proposals in front of you, you can go on to a second round of analysis. In effect you should challenge each potential supplier with questions about what the other firms recommended and they did not. "Why can't you do . . . . . ? XYZ can!" This will make each candidate think. Perhaps they will convince you such and such a feature really is not needed, or would not be used, or their own system can accomplish the same result with slightly different inputs and outputs. In short, you really want to develop an understanding of the strengths and weaknesses of each vendor.

All other things being equal, should you pick the vendor with the largest market share? The positive reason for this approach might be, "Well, all the other customers can't be wrong." However, because the cost of fixed-asset software is relatively low, the high market share providers might simply have better or more aggressive sales reps.

Each of the vendors will provide you with a list of existing customers who you can call. The trouble with this is that they will have "cherry-picked" the people to call, selecting satisfied customers, and omitting dissatisfied customers. Rather than asking for some references, ask to get a list of the five most *recent* customers, those still going through the pains of a conversion. Then you may be able to deduce which vendors are really providing the best service; this of course is important because there is not a vendor in the world who does not promise "service." You want to understand any differences between prior promises and current reality among recent customers.

With respect to the actual capabilities of each of the competitive systems, certain questions regarding your own unique situation will come to mind in the course of this evaluation. You will want to evaluate the competitors on how they handle the issues that are of importance to you. Since each company is unique, we cannot provide a checklist here of such items on a "one size fits all" basis.

Should you hire a consulting firm to help in the evaluation? That may appear to be the easy way out. "Let him ask the tough questions, summarize the answers, and give us a single recommendation." This is not recommended. If *you* do not have the time or the interest to understand what the software *should* do, and what it *can* do, how will the consultant? Where will the consultant obtain his input on your unique and specific requirements? By the time you educate the consultant, it will be quicker (and less expensive) to do this yourself.

We recommend a modest trial for the two or three "finalists" you consider for adoption. The key individual in the final selection should *not* be the IT manager. It should *not* be the corporate controller. It *should* be the property accountant who will be working with the software day in and day out. Let him or her make the choice. Today's software, almost irrespective of vendor, is going to perform whatever you need; if it cannot, that most likely will be easily resolved.

We cannot stress enough that selection of the software is the easiest and least expensive part of getting true internal control over fixed assets. In fact, the real differences between and among the major software vendors may be relatively unimportant. The real cost, and management effort, is going to be understanding what assets you actually have, where they are located, and what you will do with assets on the existing register you cannot find, and what to do with assets you do have that do not appear to be on the register.

Having said this, perhaps one of the areas of inquiry during the selection process would be how much in the way of resources the vendor will provide, postacquisition. Some hand-holding should be expected, and beyond that level you should expect to pay for help from the vendor in implementation. How much time, and at what rate per hour, do you think you will use? Then triple that estimate and you may be close!

ASSIGN RESPONSIBILITY FOR IMPLEMENTATION AND BEYOND

"Internal control is a process effected by an entity's Board of Directors, management, and other personnel designed to provide reasonable assurance regarding the achievement of objectives. . . . Internal control is applicable to all business processes. Internal control should be built 'into' and not 'onto' the various business processes."[1]

In practice, with reference to PP&E, individual managers must take responsibility for meeting the requirements of the control system of fixed assets. What is "everybody's business is nobody's business" is never more true than in PP&E.

You can have the best software system in the world; every asset can be tagged and accounted for, lives and depreciation methods that have been chosen fully comply with tax and accounting requirements. But that nirvana, if ever achieved, is valid for only one day, unless all actions affecting PP&E are recorded properly in the system, *as they occur*. In turn this means that the property accountant, responsible for maintaining the records, has to be informed of *all* additions, sales and transfers, and dispositions. It is totally unrealistic to assume that a relatively low-level person in the accounting or tax department can keep on top of everything impacting PP&E.

Managers *must* be held responsible for communicating the appropriate information at the time something happens. It is all too easy for a shop superintendent to say to himself,

"I am up to my rear end in alligators and I just don't have time to fill out the paperwork related to the transfer of that milling machine. And anyhow the depreciation charges will continue whether or not I inform accounting about the move. Let X, the property accountant, himself come down to the shop floor and fill out his own damned paperwork. I have better things to do with my time!"

Does that sound familiar? It should, because this is the root cause of lack of control over PP&E. Things happen in a remote office or factory and there is no way for the accountant responsible for property records to find out. No accountant can be all over the company monitoring what is going on.

No, the responsibility belongs to department managers to initiate the flow of information. Performance measurement is the only tool management has to ensure that procedures regarding PP&E are followed.

CHARGING DEPARTMENTS WILL ENSURE INDIVIDUAL RESPONSIBILITY

"What gets measured gets done." This somewhat cynical saying unfortunately has a strong element of truth to it. If internal control means anything, it requires knowing where things are *supposed* to be and then assuring that they *are* there. But as mentioned before, the appropriate information often is not provided to those who are keeping the records. Consequently, the basic records will be wrong, or at least inadequate. At that point it is impossible for a CFO to assert in an SOX (Sarbanes-Oxley) filing that PP&E is under control.

So, how do you get line managers to take personal responsibility for the accuracy of the records related to PP&E under their control? By stating the issue this way, the answer almost becomes self-evident.

Department heads must be responsible for the assets charged to their department; that is, we start by assuming the property record's location information is correct. Periodic audit of a sample of assets should then be undertaken. If an asset charged to a department is not found there, the book value of that asset should be charged as a period expense to the department in question.

Such a charge to the unit's profit and loss is almost guaranteed to get results, inasmuch as the charge will stand out on any variance report because there will have been no corresponding budget entry.

The immediate response from the affected manager to such a charge on the monthly financial statement will be for her to go to one of her assistants to "find out what happened to that specific asset and send the information to the accounting department so the charge will go away!" Guess what, albeit months or years later, the accounting department will have been informed that the subject asset was transferred or moved to another floor, building, department, or unit and the expense charge removed.

Once operating managers realize that they will be penalized if they do *not* inform the property record department, it will soon become second nature for an individual in each department informally to be appointed the custodian of the asset record information for that unit. There is no better incentive than charging a department, on an unbudgeted basis, for "missing" assets.

What this requires is a periodic inventory sampling of high-dollar value assets; it is not necessary for this to be done on a company-wide simultaneous basis. It can be performed on a cycle basis by internal auditing or the property accountant.

Charging a manager's monthly statement with the dollar value of a missing item will highlight the need for proper information flow, to an extent much more than most managers would like. Questions will be asked, and the only answer has to be, "Well we forgot to fill out the paperwork. This won't happen again." In fact it may result in a request by many managers to, "Please send me a listing of the assets you show in my department. I want to check they are still here, and resolve any differences." This is perhaps an ideal response, but represents the first step in having managers take responsibility for the assets reported to be in their department.

Once managers are willing to accept the property record as representing where things *should* be, then they will have an incentive to notify the accounting department with changes. With regard to transfers between departments, putting the burden on the *sending* department is far better than putting it on the receiving department. The sending department will be charged for the asset if it is not there, whereas the receiving department has no real incentive for doing anything. That is all right, getting the first half of the transfer recorded properly is all that is necessary for good control.

While we have been talking about transfers, and these are more common, any disposals, usually through trade-in, scrap, or sale should also be followed up. The accounting department can take the initiative here, because they will be informed about new acquisitions, and that always raises the question about trade-ins. Scrap sales generate cash, so cash receipts from asset sales can be forwarded to the property accountant for the proper entries to be made.

If accurate information is supplied to the accounting department, maintaining a good property register is straightforward. In the absence of current information, the task becomes impossible; the result over a few periods is that a claim that there is internal control over fixed assets is going to be impossible to support. Good records can lead to good control. No records are guaranteed to lead to no control.

 ## RETURN ON INVESTMENT ANALYSIS

One advantage of holding line management responsible for the assets under their control is the ability to determine a realistic return on assets (ROA) employed. If a company knows what assets are involved in what operating units, it is simple to calculate an ROA for producing departments. If you have one physical location, and essentially one product or product line, an ROA analysis does little to enhance cash flow or income.

However, if a company has diverse operations, say, for example, both a pharmaceutical and a consumer unit, determining the appropriate ROA can help in future capital budgeting and asset allocations. Calculation of ROA of course encompasses far more than just PP&E. Net working capital may be equally, if not more, important in some situations. Nonetheless, the dollar amount of invested capital tied up in PP&E can easily be 20% or more of total assets.

Requests for additional capital expenditures (capex) almost always exceed the availability of funds; hence the prevalence of capital budgeting and associated management approval requirements for capex. One of the key metrics, before approving additional investments in new assets, should be an analysis of how well existing assets are being used.

A simple calculation of net operating income for a unit, divided by total assets employed, may not be particularly meaningful on a standalone basis. ROA analysis, however, can be extremely useful and provide management insight if they are carried out over a period of years. What is the trend? If the trend is negative, ROA is declining, this should spark much more detailed analysis.

Comparing your firm's ROA with that of direct competitors, assuming they are publicly traded and the information is available, may or may not be as useful as you might think at first. The reason is that if your ROA is lower than your competitor, just what can you do about it?

You have your business model, and they have theirs. You cannot suddenly adopt their business model and hope to achieve their ROA. What you can do with the comparative information, and those of us in the valuation business usually do look at this, is to analyze *why* they are doing better. This will probably stimulate some ideas, although it is unrealistic to think that any sudden improvement is likely, or even possible.

When discussing ROA, many professors make the argument that you should not use book value (original cost less accumulated depreciation) but it is far superior to utilize the true *fair value* of the assets employed. The theoretical benefits of a fair value analysis are clear.

But, in practice, there are usually relatively small differences between fair value and book value, and as discussed in Chapter 12, they often tend to offset each other. Inflation has caused replacement costs to increase, but overly short lives for depreciation go the other way. Fully depreciated assets still in use overstate the ROA on total assets employed, since the zero book value of a fully depreciated asset drops out of the calculation.

Offsetting this understatement is that technological changes, think new IT equipment, mean that the fair value of some equipment presently in use may be less than their stated book value.

With the possible exception of land and some buildings acquired many years ago, in our valuation work we rarely see vast discrepancies between fair value and book value. The conclusion should be clear. Do not spend time trying to determine the fair value of assets for any sort of ROA analysis. Using book values will be directionally accurate, and will certainly allow you to discern any results that call for further study.

A final word on this subject. As valuation specialists we see an almost unlimited number of reasons why clients want or need information about the fair value (accounting) or fair market value (tax and business) of the assets they own, are about to buy, or want to sell. In over 40 years, however, this writer has *never* been employed by a client to determine valuations that will be used solely, or even primarily, for ROA purposes or analysis. Stick with book values, and if the information in this book is applied so that the property records are themselves accurate, use of book value will be totally satisfactory.

 ## SUMMARY

Assets, and asset records, do not take care of themselves. Passively waiting for appropriate information to arrive in the accounting department, if that is where the property register is kept, does not work. Line managers seemingly always have "something better to do with their time" than fill out paperwork on asset transfers and disposals.

Yet without prompt and accurate information the property register will never be accurate, and true internal control over PP&E will be lacking. Some incentive must be applied in order to get line managers to report changes in PP&E. The method recommended is to have spot audits by internal audit or the property accountant to check that high-dollar value assets are physically present where the record suggests they should be. Any asset not found on such an audit should be charged to the expense of the department affected.

Internal control over fixed assets, as the saying goes, is not brain surgery. A competent accountant with the right information can do a good job, and the CFO can then confidently sign an SOX certification. In the absence of current information about transfers, dispositions, and retirements, internal control will be lacking and a CFO who signs, despite this situation, is asking for trouble.

 NOTE

1. www.Big4Guy.com, [August 20, 2010]. Sarbanes Oxley and COSO—Definition of Internal Control

4

Depreciation and Amortization for Books and Taxes

THERE IS ONE OVERRIDING principle that a reader should take away from this chapter. Depreciation methods, amortization lives, fixed-asset lives, and salvage values *can* and probably *should* differ between financial reporting and taxes. The Internal Revenue Service (IRS) will review that each taxpayer has identified the specific *tax* accounting requirements for Property, Plant, and Equipment (PP&E) and that the regulations are followed. With regard to PP&E the IRS does not care what a taxpayer does for financial reporting. Only with LIFO (last in, first out) is there a requirement for conformity between book accounting and tax accounting.

Similarly, for financial reporting, how a taxpayer chooses lives, salvage values, and depreciation methods for taxes in no way needs to govern what the company does for its own financial statements. Auditors, reviewing internal controls, will assure themselves that the client is following its own written accounting policies; nothing in generally accepted accounting principles (GAAP) explicitly requires certain specific lives or depreciation methods, much less a single salvage value. As was shown in Chapter 3, current fixed-asset accounting software easily handles differing tax and financial reporting software.

In short, there need be no connection between tax accounting for PP&E and financial reporting of the same assets. As was mentioned in Chapter 2, many companies *choose* to use both the *same* lives and *same* depreciation methods for both books and taxes. But this choice, while frequently made, is not based on any specific accounting or tax requirements.

There is one reason for having the same lives and methods, and that is to preclude the GAAP requirement that deferred taxes be set up for differences between tax accounting and financial accounting. All other things being equal, most companies prefer to minimize deferred taxes if for no other reason than simplifying month-end accounting. The subject of deferred tax accounting is beyond the scope of this book on internal controls. But the slight increase in accounting effort to handle deferred tax accounting is almost always worth the effort to improve overall financial reporting.

Financial managers attempt to maximize after-tax cash flow, and as a generalization utilize the most aggressive, yet acceptable, tax policies which will improve cash flow. This comes at the cost of potentially incurring small increased effort. Keep in mind that deferred tax accounting involves reporting and audit requirements for deferred tax assets and liabilities that are on the balance sheet.

For *tax* purposes, asset lives have essentially been developed by Congress and the IRS; for taxes IRS Publication 946[1] provides exhaustive detail. In addition to prescribed lives the Internal Revenue Code also lays out acceptable depreciation methods. The combination for taxes of specified lives and specified depreciation methods means that if companies follow the advice in this book, and determine depreciation for financial reports separately, there are bound to be accounting differences between books and taxes. In turn, these differences will require calculation and the reporting of deferred tax assets and liabilities. Most companies can handle differences in tax and book reporting and the concomitant deferred tax accounting, but smaller firms may want to ask their financial advisors which way to go.

INTERNAL CONTROL FOR DEPRECIABLE TANGIBLE ASSETS

Note: Land is the only tangible asset that is *not* depreciated, so this section covers *all* PP&E including machinery, IT assets, office furniture and fixtures, and buildings, but not land.

Books have been written about internal control and most publicly traded companies issue a report on their internal controls. We are not repeating the broad generalizations that govern the subject, our discussion is limited to factors unique to PP&E.

There are basically two things required in order to meet independent standards of internal control for PP&E:

1. Proper accounting for acquisition, transfer, and disposition of PP&E.
2. Monitoring that the accounting records accurately reflect underlying economics.

DETERMINING USEFUL LIVES WHENEVER NEW ASSETS ARE ACQUIRED

There is a very easy way to tell if you have been assigning appropriate lives to PP&E in your company. Take the existing file and sort it by net book value (original cost less accumulated depreciation). The chances are very high that there will be a substantial number of assets that have been fully depreciated, that show zero net book value, or only salvage value, and the assets are still present and still in use.

By definition, then, a fully depreciated asset still in use had too short a life initially assigned. Of course, circumstances change. It is hard to project out 10, 15, or even 20 years out into the future. It is much easier simply to use the same life required by the IRS for financial reporting. Most companies, in practice, do exactly this.

The rules in GAAP for setting lives and computing depreciation for financial reporting are not prescriptive, unlike the IRS rules. You simply are supposed to assign a life that corresponds to your best estimate of the expected useful (economic) life. If you really expect a salvage value, that is to be set up; salvage values affect depreciation by reducing the total allowable amount charged to expense over the assets' lives. Many companies do not assign a salvage value, anticipating that by the time an asset is replaced it will have little or no commercial value at that time.

Factors to Be Considered in Setting Lives

Experience has shown that very few assets truly wear out, that is, they have to be taken out of service because they simply cannot be held together. When was the last time you saw a worn-out desk?

Unfortunately, individuals in an accounting department who make decisions concerning the lives of assets are all too familiar with one type of machinery and equipment, the private car that does have a short life due to physical wear and tear. Automobiles, however, are not typical of PP&E in the average company, Hertz and Avis excepted.

As we all know, cars do wear out, and after 150,000 or 200,000 miles most owners decide to buy a new car, they trade in the old auto, because the cost of repairs is getting out of hand. Physical depreciation on productive assets used in the business world does exist, but to a much lesser degree than is usually thought of.

In a production environment preventive maintenance is carried out, while for office furniture and fixtures there is usually little actual wear and tear. Technology assets, computers and related assets, suffer functional obsolescence and thus may have a short economic life. But a 15-year-old computer will probably still perform the functions for which it was designed originally. It is just that developments in new technology rapidly outdate or obsolete older equipment.

Look at buildings, and you see a much different story. The IRS calls for a 39-year life for buildings and many managers then use that life for financial reporting. Taking 2011 as a measure, this would suggest that most buildings constructed prior to 1972 were supposedly at the end of their life. Obviously, many, if not most, structures used for business, retail, wholesale, transportation, and manufacturing last far longer than 39 years. The record, and we do not recommend this as a comparable to be used for financial reporting, is Gothic Cathedrals. There are many churches in Europe still being used for their original purpose, in many cases 600 or more years after construction.

The assets that color individual understanding of asset lives are personal computers and consumer electronics. How many different computers have you had in the last 20 or 25 years? Many individuals probably have upgraded every two or three years, meaning that a two- or three-year life would have been appropriate for financial reporting.

Computers do not wear out. A computer from 15 years ago will still perform all the functions today it was capable of then. It may not be able to handle the "bloated" software now in common usage, but the word processing program from that era will still turn out more than acceptable reports on the computer from that era.

Truth be told, today's word processing software does very little more than the programs did from that period. Human typing skill has not changed and that is the real limiting factor, not computer speed or software features. Now today's software for fixed assets probably would not run on a 15-year-old computer, but any of today's programs on today's personal computers undoubtedly will be completely functional ten or even 15 years from today.

For valuation specialists who deal in machinery and equipment, much of their professional expertise lies in the determination of remaining useful lives. Keep in mind that the valuation of an asset is itself a function of how long it will continue to be used. Thus, the same asset, if it will become economically or functionally obsolete in five years, will have a lower "value" today than if the same asset could be used for the next 20 years. The value of the asset and the life of the asset are really the two sides of the same coin.

As a generalization, productive assets used in business do not wear out! Very few current capital expenditures are actually to replace existing assets on a one for one basis.

Before getting into the details of setting lives for specific assets or types of assets, let us examine carefully why new assets are acquired. Many, if not most, larger companies have formal capital expenditure approval systems. Companies establish a budget for capital expenditures for the year, then individuals submit requests with justification; a higher level of management then approves or disapproves the request. Companies have a number of different categories into which they slot capital expenditures, and some of the most common are:

- *Mandatory.* Mandatory capital expenditures (capex) encompass health, safety, and environmental projects which have to be done irrespective of their return on investment (ROI). For this category the usual economic analysis as to future benefits and cash flow is usually omitted. If the Environmental Protection Agency tells you to clean up a site, and you have exhausted your legal defenses, you probably are going to have to spend the money.
- *Expansion (existing products).* Expansion projects are usually justified on the basis of incremental profits expected from the increased sales of current products that are already doing well. Inasmuch as these are usually based on current production methods, only scaling them up, the types of assets to be acquired are familiar.
- *New product.* Capex for new products involves more risk and possibly unknown technology. The ultimate success of any new venture is far less secure than the expansion of presently successful activities. For this reason most companies have a higher hurdle rate for this type of proposal.
- *Cost reduction.* Cost reduction projects usually involve a "make" versus "buy" decision, and if you can do something yourself, and hence not pay a supplier, it is possible for profits to increase. The success of such projects is quite certain because you already know the volumes at which the cost

reduction project will run. What may not be as certain is whether or not you can "make" at lower cost than your existing supplier can. Thus there is some risk in terms of making the project work.

- *Replacement.* Replacement projects are where existing equipment simply is worn out and it is uneconomical to try and fix it. This is the phenomenon we as consumers have with cars and consumer electronics and appliances. After six years it is probably time to trade in your car and in ten years it probably is time to get a new washing machine. These are what we call "one for one" or replacement decisions, and for industry they simply permit the existing business to go along at current levels. But in practice these are fairly rare.

It is our observation over many years in the business world that there is a very low percentage of replacement capex compared to the other four categories. Good maintenance can keep equipment working for many years. This of course is why companies have so many fully depreciated assets physically still in use. The original life fell short of the actual economic utility.

The point of this brief digression is to put into perspective that there are few replacements, relative to all other capex. Unlike individuals who get a new washing machine after ten years, most production managers and plant engineers can get 20, 30, or more years usage out of production equipment.

The conclusion we draw from this analysis is that companies should adopt a new approach to setting financial reporting lives for new capex. In Chapter 8 we take another look at the actual remaining lives for assets already on the books. But for *new* acquisitions, the time to start is now, from here forward.

 ## CHOOSING ACCOUNTING LIVES

The first place to start is to look at the existing file of fully depreciated assets, those with either zero book value or salvage value only. Take a sample of those items that had too short a life originally assigned, then determine what the real economic life is likely to be. This will involve dialog between the fixed-asset accountant and the appropriate production or IT managers responsible for actually using the asset.

We hate to say it, but the level of knowledge about manufacturing processes for most financial workers ranges from abysmal to none. Accountants really should not be setting expected lives at all—other than for tax purposes. For financial reporting, where the underlying economics should govern, accountants and auditors really are fooling themselves if they believe they know enough to set lives appropriate for actual intended use.

For *replacement* capex it would be appropriate to use as a life for the newly acquired asset, the actual elapsed time between the acquisition of the original asset and the current date when it is being replaced. If the new asset replaces a similar asset acquired 25 years ago, then assign a 25-year life to the new asset. There have been many studies that suggest simply projecting what has happened in the past is the best estimate of the future. If it rained today, the best forecast for tomorrow is that it will rain then. This does not mean that it will rain continuously from here, but for a one-day forecast it may beat any other forecast. Assigning a 25-year life to the new asset on the basis that the old asset lasted 25 years is as supportable, if not more so, than any other choice.

Taking this approach, in effect lengthening the accounting lives of re-placement assets, will have no effect on cash flow, but *will have the impact of reporting increased income.* Earnings before interest, taxes, depreciation, and amortization (EBITDA), as well as earnings before depreciation, is also not affected by the choice of accounting lives for calculating depreciation.

But having correct economic depreciation will give a better picture of true profitability. Many accountants have been brought up with an expect-ation that they should always be conservative. In this context, with respect to depreciation expense, conservative is assumed to be that the faster you write off an asset the better. Why it is better, however, has never been made clear, at least to the author.

Understating profitability (the result of overly aggressive depreciation charges) may lead to incorrect product pricing, as well as incorrect financial analysis of the relative profitability of different product lines. This is a point made strongly in cost accounting courses in colleges and universities. Choosing economic reality is usually trumped by the feeling that "it is good to be conservative and even better to be overly conservative." That bad decisions may arise is not contemplated by the desire for conservatism. But the actual rule for depreciation is very straightforward, as shown in Accounting Stan-dards Codification (ASC) 360-10-35-3:

> 35-3: "Depreciation expense in financial statements for an asset shall be determined based on the asset's useful life."

It does not say to choose a life based on the Internal Revenue Code. It does not say to choose a life that will write the asset off as quickly as possible. It does say exactly what we are recommending. Use the *expected* useful life.

Without parsing the words too closely "useful life" refers to the period over which the asset will perform its expected function. Thus, what we have to do is anticipate *economic* lives in order to determine accounting lives.

HOW VALUATION SPECIALISTS DETERMINE ECONOMIC LIVES

In valuing an existing factory full of equipment, the appraiser attempts to determine for each significant asset how much of the real useful life has been used up or expired and how much remains. The thought process looks at the economics of the operation, taking into consideration current maintenance policies, and how well they are practiced. Machinery and equipment appraisers typically disregard accounting lives and book balances (original cost less accumulated financial depreciation).

This actually is common sense, once one considers this. If you maintain your car, changing the oil every 5,000 miles, and so forth, the car will last a lot longer than if you simply fill it up with gas and drive it until it falls apart. The same holds true in a manufacturing environment. Preventive maintenance is the "gold standard"; machinery and equipment appraisers are trained to evaluate what a company is doing, irrespective of what a written policy says is *supposed* to happen.

Take airplanes, where preventive maintenance is scrupulously followed, occasional complaints by the Federal Aviation Administration (FAA) notwithstanding. The U.S. Air Force is still flying bombers built in the 1950s and actually relying on them for much of the United States' offensive capability. Some observers have pointed out that over the 50-year period virtually 100% of the original aircraft has been physically replaced, so perhaps it is semantics to say that the original bomber is now 50 years old. But if it is not the original aircraft, thoroughly maintained, then what is it?

The point here is that with good maintenance assets can, and do, last a lot longer than is usually thought. This has implications for the lives assigned to new asset acquisitions. What we recommend is simple and straightforward: Instead of an accountant setting the economic lives, have the owner or user of the asset determine the life. That is, the individual or department, which will bear the depreciation charge. Keep in mind that depreciation expense, no matter how often people call it a "noncash charge" does represent actual expense associated with the original purchase. The cost of an asset has to be reflected in the selling price of the assets made from that asset.

Perhaps the simplest example would be an excavating contractor who uses a Caterpillar bulldozer. Most contractors determine a "cost per hour of operation" and then charge that to jobs and use that charge in their cost estimating and pricing. Assets have a cost, and the per-unit cost is a function of the expected future use. Underestimating that use, or useful life, throws off all cost and profit analyses.

Therefore, go to the most knowledgeable people in the company, the users of the assets. This means that for computers and related gear, go to the head of IT. For buildings, ask the real estate manager. For machinery and equipment the experts are in production and maintenance, not sitting in the accounting department. In fact the only asset that accountants should determine the life of is office furniture and HP calculators! And the latter should have been charged to expense, not capitalized.

 ## DETERMINING LIVES FOR INTANGIBLE ASSETS

For tax purposes, the answer is crystal clear. Internal Revenue Code §197 specifies, without any distinctions, that *all* intangible assets, including goodwill, are to be amortized over 15 years. There is no choice: 15 years, no more and no less. This was put into the Code at the behest of the IRS, and agreed to by industry, to eliminate the interminable fights over lives that took place prior to §197's enactment.

The IRS had not allowed goodwill to be amortized for tax purposes, but did allow amortization for intangible assets where the taxpayer could demonstrate a definitive life and a definitive value. Thus, there was pressure by taxpayers to try and carve out of goodwill any number of identifiable intangibles and valuation firms were hired to value these and determine a specific life.

The IRS, seeing tax revenues drain away, almost invariably challenged these intangibles, such as customer relationships or assembled workforce, and alleged they were simply components of goodwill and hence *not* amortizable. The disputes ended up in court, consuming real resources in what was essentially a zero-sum game between taxpayers and the IRS. Finally, both sides threw in the towel and agreed that 15 years for everything, including goodwill, was a reasonable compromise.

This 15-year rule does have some unexpected consequences, however. A five-year noncompete contract obviously has no value after five years. But under today's tax rules such an asset still must be amortized over 15 years.

Similarly, while goodwill is never amortized for financial reporting under GAAP, it is given a 15-year life for tax purposes.

Where lives for intangible assets do become critical is in financial reporting. Goodwill is never amortized, following issuance of Statement of Financial Accounting Standards (SFAS) 157 Fair Value, now ASC 820. In exchange for getting rid of "Pooling of Interests" accounting the Financial Accounting Standards Board (FASB) permitted goodwill to be tested periodically for impairment. Absent an impairment, however, goodwill is not amortized; further it is treated as having what is called an "indefinite" life. Important to this discussion is that indefinite does not mean "infinite," it merely means that we do not know today when the useful life may end. This distinction becomes important and is discussed ahead.

Nonamortization of goodwill, following a business combination, is highly prized by CFOs and controllers, who thereby do not have a charge reducing earnings and hence earnings per share (EPS). This initial determination of the amount of goodwill occurs in an allocation of purchase price. Since most other intangible assets with a specific life do have to be amortized, and such amortization reduces EPS, financial officers usually want as much of the total purchase price allocated to goodwill and as little as possible to amortizable intangibles.

Now we get to the critical element of this section. What is the appropriate life to be assigned to specific intangible assets? The answer "it depends" is not particularly helpful. The rule that is supposed to be followed is to assign a life for reporting purposes that is commensurate with the useful life or expected utility of the asset, just as with fixed assets. This certainly leads immediately to the next question, of how do you determine the useful life of an asset? We mentioned above a five-year covenant not to compete, and the useful life would in most cases be determined as five years. Similarly, a patent with seven years remaining before expiration would ordinarily be assigned a seven-year life.

These examples beg the question for assets that do not have clearly defined or delineated terms until expiration. The issue here is that the assigned life at times directly affects the value. As a simple example, if in an allocation of purchase price you assume a five-year life for royalty income, say on a software system the target company licenses to customers, then the value of the license might be $1 million. But if you assume the revenue stream could last eight years, the value might be $1.2 million. The length of an income stream directly corresponds (on a discounted basis) to the anticipated life.

In terms of internal controls, the main subject of this book, it is critical that the estimates of lives of intangibles be assessed as accurately as possible.

Overassessment, putting too long a life and hence too high a value, is likely to result in future impairment charges, which no financial officer (not to mention top management and security analysts or shareholders) likes to see. It is true that a longer life does reduce the charge to expense in the early years, at the expense of having the amortization charge go on for a long period of time.

However, deliberately underestimating the life of the intangible, and hence underestimating the value of the asset risks putting too much of the purchase price into goodwill. While not directly impacting short-run EPS, an overstatement of goodwill may cause an impairment charge for goodwill. Inasmuch as many observers think that in 60 to 70% of M&A (mergers and acquisitions) transactions the buyer has overpaid, the risk of a goodwill impairment charge should not be dismissed out of hand. As was seen in the 2008–2009 downturn, with stock prices depressed, many companies were forced to take unanticipated goodwill impairment charges. We have seen a number of instances where the goodwill impairment charge was higher than it need to have been because of prior errors in correctly estimating the lives (and hence the amount) of amortizable intangibles.

Also, at least a word of warning. Putting more of a purchase price into goodwill, to reduce depreciation and amortization charges, risks very close scrutiny by the Securities and Exchange Commission (SEC) and public accountants. The SEC is particularly vigilant in this area, and does not hesitate to ask companies why such a high percentage of the purchase price was assigned to goodwill. In effect, they are asking why did you buy that company, what did you think you were getting. Was it products? Research? Customers? The questions can become pretty pointed.

One suggestion for purchase price allocations should be kept in mind. In many instances companies are permitted to assign an indefinite life to *trade names*. Remember that when an indefinite life is assigned, there is no annual depreciation charge. Consequently, many companies believe that the trade names they acquired in an M&A transaction truly have an indefinite life–and no amortization is required. Unfortunately, as a number of our clients have found out, too late, buyers often stop using acquired trade names, or minimize the marketing resources devoted to the trade name.

Common sense suggests that when marketing resources are reduced, the value of any trade name, or product line, is similarly diminished. The impairment test for indefinite life assets is materially different, and far more stringent, than that for amortizable assets. One has to determine the current fair value of a trade name each year if no life has been assigned. Then if sales of the product/product line go down there is almost certainly going to be a required impairment charge. However, if a definite life had been assigned, say 30 years, and sales drop off because of reduced marketing expenditures (or any other reason for that matter) the impairment test is quite easy to pass. Right or wrong, the FASB has mandated that the impairment test for amortizable assets, both tangible and intangible be based on *un*discounted future cash flows; this test is usually met so our clients have experienced few impairment charges for trade names that are being amortized.

CHANGING LIVES AND DEPRECIATION FOR EXISTING ASSETS

Often it becomes obvious that an asset will last either a shorter, or longer, time than was originally contemplated. Here is what GAAP says:

> *35-22* When a long-lived asset (asset group) is tested for recoverability, it also may be necessary to review depreciation estimates and methods as required by Topic 250 or the amortization period as required by Topic 350. Paragraphs 250-10-45-17 through 45-20 and 250-10-50-4 address the accounting for changes in estimates, including changes in the method of depreciation
>
> *50-4* The effect on income from continuing operations, net income (or other appropriate captions of changes in the applicable net assets or performance indicator), and any related per-share amounts of the current period shall be disclosed for a change in estimate that affects several future periods, such as a change in service lives of depreciable assets. Disclosure of those effects is not necessary for estimates made each period in the ordinary course of accounting for items such as uncollectible accounts or inventory obsolescence; however, disclosure is required if the effect of a change in the estimate is material. When an entity effects a change in estimate by changing an accounting principle, the disclosures required by paragraphs 250-10-50-1 through 50-3 also are required. If a change in estimate does not have a material effect in the period of change but is reasonably certain to have a material effect in later periods, a description of that change in estimate shall be disclosed whenever the financial statements of the period of change are presented

Inasmuch as we believe that most companies are using lives that are too short, it might pay to study the impact of lengthening lives. As noted previously, of course, it would be necessary to have footnote disclosure of the impact of the change. Making this change on a wholesale basis is probably not for the faint of heart, but there will be very sound support for the move, merely by looking at the fully depreciated assets, and assets that are within a year or two of becoming fully depreciated.

If the assets are going to be used for more years than was originally set forth, it would appear to be better internal control, working with your auditing firm and perhaps a valuation firm, to accomplish the task and explain, so that security analysts do not draw the wrong opinion.

 ## LEASING AS A WAY TO UTILIZE DEPRECIATION

Companies with net operating losses (NOL) can often not take advantage of the deduction for the current allowable depreciation expense. If you have an NOL that will likely carry forward for several years, there is no point in increasing tax losses by throwing in depreciation. However, the IRS does not allow you to "skip" depreciation for a year or two, whether you can use it or not. Depreciation for taxes must be taken, irrespective of the impact on profit or loss.

There are, however, many companies that *can* use depreciation because they are in a favorable profit, and hence tax-paying, condition. Nature abhors a vacuum, and unutilized tax depreciation in fact has value to such taxpayers. This is the logic behind much equipment leasing.

It is beyond the scope of this book to go into leasing, inasmuch as many long books on leasing have already been published. But if a company has NOL a good way of minimizing the impact would be to examine the economics of equipment leasing. If the lessor can use the depreciation that you cannot use, this can often be translated into an effective lower interest cost.

 ## SUMMARY

A key point of this chapter, and for the book as a whole, is that depreciation expense for any asset, or group of assets, should be determined based on the expected economic life. Simply using the same life for financial reporting as recommended by the IRS will cause assets to be depreciated too quickly. This, in turn, has an impact on reported net income, albeit not to EBITDA.

Companies can develop reasonable estimates for lives to be assigned to newly acquired assets by reviewing actual usage of existing assets. Assets still in use, but fully written off, represent past errors in the estimated life, an error which need not be repeated.

Tax lives and depreciation methods have been developed to meet social and economic needs of the economy as a whole; they were not developed based on actual or expected economic utility. Financial reporting companies must cut the tie between tax and financial depreciation.

 NOTE

1. IRS Publication 946 can be referenced at www.IRS.gov.

5

Impairment Testing

TESTING FOR THE IMPAIRMENT of assets (both tangible and intangible) is not only a generally accepted accounting principle (GAAP) requirement but absolutely essential in terms of internal control. It is critical that the real value of assets never be overstated. Keeping overvalued assets on the balance sheet misleads management, not to mention outside users of financial statements such as creditors and investors. Yet, as will be seen, there is often great reluctance to recognize impairment charges when they are required by GAAP and internal control.

The reason is simple. All impairment charges (with the possible exception of valuations of certain financial instruments which are not covered in this book) result in a charge to expense, which leads to a reduction in reported net income. We have yet to meet a CFO who wants to report less income to creditors and shareholders, disregarding for the moment the impact of impairment charges on taxable income and hence income taxes payable.

As a generalization while GAAP requires impairment testing at least annually, relatively few such charges made for financial statements have any effect on taxable income. So, in a sense, impairment charges when required and taken represent "All Pain, No Gain." Nonetheless, no matter how painful, impairment testing is required and unfortunate results, no matter how unexpected, must be reflected in audited financial statements.

Controllers and CFOs, as well as CEOs and audit committees, should understand the methodology used in the development of impairment valuations. At times it is possible to anticipate future impairment charges–this does not make the pain go away but at least precludes surprises.

Impairment testing, often considered routine, is actually far from simple. To start with, there are in practice three separate impairment testing approaches required by GAAP. They must be performed in the proper order. Further, impairment testing is almost always carefully reviewed by outside auditors, and for public companies, often by the Securities and Exchange Commission (SEC).

Impairment must be tested at least once a year for all values shown at current or fair value. Further, the Financial Accounting Standards Board (FASB) also requires additional impairment testing of Property, Plant, and Equipment (PP&E) as and when what they refer to as "impairment indicators" are present. Impairment indicators, as laid out in FASB Codification Topic 360-10, really are little more than common sense. In theory, you do not have to test PP&E unless there is a reason that suggests impairment is possible. While we show the actual rules below, the best way to think of it, is "I know it when I see it." Put another way, "If you think that some of your PP&E may be impaired, it probably is."

The following is the portion of GAAP that specifically spells out the circumstances when an impairment may be indicated, with our [comments] and emphases appended:

"When to Test a Long-Lived Asset for Recoverability

35-21 A long-lived asset (asset group) shall be tested for recoverability whenever events or changes in circumstances indicate that its carrying amount may not be recoverable. The following are examples of such events or changes in circumstances:

   a. A significant decrease in the market price of a long-lived asset (asset group) [Rare]
   b. A significant adverse change in the extent or manner in which a long-lived asset (asset group) is being used or in its physical condition [Relatively rare]
   c. A significant adverse change in legal factors or in the business climate that could affect the value of a long-lived asset (asset group), including an adverse action or assessment by a regulator [Common]

d. An accumulation of costs significantly in excess of the amount originally expected for the acquisition or construction of a long-lived asset (asset group) [Very rare]

e. A **current-period operating or cash flow loss** combined with a history of operating or cash flow losses or a projection or forecast that demonstrates continuing losses associated with the use of a long-lived asset (asset group) [Common]

f. A current expectation that, more likely than not, a long-lived asset (asset group) will be sold or otherwise disposed of significantly before the end of its previously estimated useful life. The term *more likely than not* refers to a level of likelihood that is more than 50%. [Infrequent]

35-22 When a long-lived asset (asset group) is tested for recoverability, it also may be necessary to review depreciation estimates and method as required by Topic 250 or the amortization period as required by Topic 350. Paragraphs 250-10-45-17 through 45-20 and 250-10-50-4 address the accounting for changes in estimates, including changes in the method of depreciation, amortization, and depletion."

For internal control to be effective a procedure must be in place to test PP&E for impairment as necessary. Remember that all intangible assets and goodwill do have to be tested each year, while for PP&E it need not be done to a specific schedule. It is easy to list the above impairment indicators in a policy manual, but determining when actually to apply one or more requires management judgment.

Based on our roughly ten years of experience with impairment testing, by far the most common reasons to make a positive determination that impairment exists relates to current or projected operating losses, often caused by "a significant adverse change in the business climate." In practice, in preparing a budget or forecast, see if losses are anticipated. Such anticipated losses may be caused by, or exacerbated by, excess carrying amounts for PP&E. In turn, this would call for formal impairment testing.

TESTING INTANGIBLE ASSETS THAT ARE NOT AMORTIZED

The easiest impairment test is that required by Topic 350, Intangibles. If an intangible asset (such as a trade name or Federal Communications Commission (FCC) license) is not being amortized, its life is considered indefinite. Indefinite life assets must be valued every year, and the test is to determine its *current* fair value. If the currently determined fair value is *less* than the amount on the books, an impairment charge is taken to reduce the carrying value to the new fair value which had just been developed. If the currently determined fair value is equal to, or greater than, the current carrying amount, then *no impairment* is present and nothing can be done. Although rare, we occasionally have a company which desires to take an impairment charge, but this is prohibited unless the test of current fair value is made and the fair value is below the book value. In other words, "voluntary" impairments are forbidden.

By the same token, one is not allowed to write-up the intangible asset to the new value. Impairment testing under U.S. GAAP is a one-way street. Sometimes this is referred to as the "roach motel" approach. Recall the old advertisement where the roach could get in but never get out. Similarly you can take an impairment charge, but never get out and reverse the expense charge if things have improved, at least back up to the original value. Interestingly, under International Financial Reporting Standards (IFRS) such write-ups are permitted. So, if the United States were to adopt IFRS, this is one of the major changes that would take place.

The impairment test for indefinite life assets, that is, seeing what the current estimate is of the fair value of the asset, requires a valuation of that specific asset. What is the proper methodology for this test?

Inasmuch as every intangible appears on the balance sheet as a consequence of a previous business combination, it is recommended that the *same* valuation methodology be used currently as was originally used. In other words, while there is often more than one way to value an asset, companies should not pick and choose one method over another just because it might provide a better answer. Auditors do check for consistency in valuation; companies and their valuation advisors should be careful, and first, go back and obtain the original analysis and then be sure to use the same approach. There may be circumstances where the original technique is no longer applicable, but any such change should be well documented.

It should be noted that in practice there are very few intangible assets that are not being amortized. The primary asset class in this category is trade names, sometimes called brand names. Many brands have histories in excess of 100 years (e.g., Budweiser) and it would be ridiculous to start amortizing such an asset on the premise that it loses value as it gets older. Well-established brands actually increase in value over time, as long as marketing efforts are continued. For PP&E, where value is often a function of age and usage, there are few examples of values increasing over time.

For trade names, however, the more it is advertised and marketed, the higher the probability it is likely to *increase* in value. Hence the FASB, in setting up testing rules for intangible assets, recognized this economic reality. Consequently, GAAP does not *require* amortization of trade name values. The downside to not amortizing a trade name, however, can come if the company decides to either cease using it, or puts primary emphasis on a different brand and sales of the original product start to decline.

Companies should only assign an indefinite life to trade names that they are absolutely sure will be continued, short of an economic catastrophe. Good brand names do go on seemingly forever, but weaker brands tend to fall by the wayside. We have seen numerous situations where a large portion of the purchase price of a company is assigned to the acquired trade name, and no amortization is required or taken. Subsequently, the company realizes it makes little economic sense to try and maintain two separate brand names for the same or similar products or services. A rationalization of marketing expense results in the acquired brand being downgraded or eliminated. The next time the brand name is tested for impairment, lo and behold there is now a very large and perhaps unexpected charge required.

As a result of this experience many companies are now electing *not* to treat brand names or trade names as having an indefinite life. Rather they assign a long (20 to 30 years) life and take a small annual amortization charge each year. With a 20-year life this would require 5% of the original value to be written off each year, while a 30-year life would require 3.33% as an annual expense. The advantage of this certain, albeit relatively long, life is that the impairment testing no longer is based on current fair value. Rather the testing for *amortizable* intangibles, and PP&E, is governed by Topic 360. As we will see, this test is truly unique in the annals of financial analysis. This amortization approach has the effect of writing down the reported fair value of the brand, so amortization can only be recommended where there is a significant possibility that the brand will be discontinued or downgraded.

TESTING FOR IMPAIRMENT OF PROPERTY, PLANT, AND EQUIPMENT, AND AMORTIZABLE INTANGIBLES

In the 1980s many companies took impairment charges seemingly at will, often to "clear the decks" when new management came in. Other companies, seemingly with losses, refused to take any impairment charges and told their auditors "show me where it says I *have to* take an impairment charge." Of course, with nothing in GAAP directly on target, there was nothing the auditors could point to. Recognizing this as a problem, the FASB stepped into this vacuum and determined that a standardized approach to impairment testing was needed and that they would provide it.

While few corporate financial officers could object to a standardized approach to impairment testing, there was still great fear that FASB would move to adopt the dreaded fair value accounting so beloved of many academics and security analysts. If the FASB put in an impairment test that resulted in numerous charges, in each case writing the asset down to its then current fair value, this was perceived as a giant step toward full fair value accounting.

Under such a fair value accounting regime, net income would be calculated as the *difference* between beginning-of-the-year equity and end-of-the-year equity. It is not necessary to go into the problems such a system would cause; suffice it to say that at least theoretically FASB *still* prefers this approach. So far, the fears have not been realized and among the many reasons for this is that there are not enough valuation specialists in the world to determine the fair value all corporate assets every year, much less every quarter.

So fair value accounting is not currently on the horizon. But because of fears that it *might* be coming, in order to dispel unnecessary concerns among its constituents, FASB developed a unique valuation method of determining impairment through the use of *un*discounted future cash flows. As long as the sum of the future cash flows is greater than the carrying or book value of the asset, or group of assets, by definition there is no impairment charge.

At the public hearings prior to adoption of what was then Statement of Financial Accounting Standards (SFAS) 121 (superseded by SFAS 144), the author was one of the people testifying. I told them that while I understood this undiscounted cash flow test, no client had ever asked me for that information. Fifteen years later, still no client has ever asked for an analysis of *un*discounted cash flows, other than in the context of impairment testing.

The actual test is very easy to describe. You add up all the future cash flows and compare the total to the carrying value of the asset. As long as the sum of the future cash flows exceeds the carrying value, the company "passes" the test and no impairment charge has to be taken, or even can be taken voluntarily. The question immediately arises, "Well, ok, I understand, but how far into the future do I keep on estimating cash flows?" As long as the asset was deriving even $1.00 a year of positive cash flows, if you carried the test long enough every asset would "pass."

Needless to say, the FASB understood this just as clearly as did any of their constituents. The rule now in place is simple common sense: carry out the projection for the period of time equal to the major asset in the group. So if you have a building with a remaining 26-year life, you can add up the next 26 years of expected cash flows. If you have a patent with but three years remaining then you can carry out the analysis for only three years.

The more difficult part of the analysis is determining what should be the correct measure of future cash flows. The impairment test is applied only to specific assets or groups of assets, not to a business as a whole. A company may have many different product lines, and many production facilities, with lots of interactions between and among them. The rule is easier to state than to apply:

> "Determine the lowest level at which specific cash flows can be identified."

It sounds simple and straightforward, but in practice reasonable people can, and do, differ in interpreting the rule. Let us start with an easy example. You have a production line with a half dozen discrete machine tools. Virtually every piece made requires operations on two or more of the tools. Five out of six of the machines are relatively new, but there is an older lathe which is nearing the end of its useful life and requires constant maintenance, even though it still carries a substantial book value. Common sense says that the value of the lathe is undoubtedly less than book value and that therefore "it is obvious we have an impairment and should write down the carrying value of the lathe to its current fair value."

Here is a situation where the given rules give an incorrect answer, and it would be far better to have a principle that simply states "write down assets to their current fair value." But GAAP is based on rules, and the rule quoted above calls for specific cash flows to be identified. It is impractical to determine what cash flows (cash receipts from the sales of the products produced on the production line) are attributable to the lathe and what remainder of the cash flows is attributable to the remaining five pieces of equipment. We can determine the total cash flows, and the total book value of the line, but we cannot determine the cash flows attributable solely to the lathe. Hence, there would not be an impairment charge to write down the lathe to fair value.

The other end of the spectrum is easy. You have an office building in a depressed economic area. No matter how you look at it the future net cash flows (after out-of-pocket expenses like taxes, insurance, and maintenance) sum up to less than the carrying amount of that building. You then write down the building on your books, taking an impairment charge to bring the new carrying value to the current fair value of the building.

The more usual, and more complex, problems arise when there are multiple products and multiple facilities. In effect, what is called for is a sophisticated cost accounting analysis that helps determine a net cash flow, which can then be summed up over future years. It is beyond the scope of this book to provide cost accounting guidance. What can be stated is that a reasonable attempt at identifying cash flows related to a reasonable grouping of assets is all that companies should strive for and that auditors should review. Anyone who has dealt with cost allocations and cost accounting knows that precision (beloved of auditors, unfortunately) is not possible. There are many ways to allocate costs, and different allocations will produce somewhat different answers. Pick a reasonable one, and let the consequences fall out.

Based on a lot of experience in this area, it is a safe generalization that while impairment testing is often required, the number of actual impairment charges based on Accounting Standards Codification (ASC) 360 is relatively few. The reason is that the FASB's fear of causing too many charges, which led them to develop this *un*discounted cash flow approach, has in practice worked out the way they expected. There are relatively few impairment charges, even though common sense sometimes suggests otherwise.

 ## REVIEWING LIVES FOR ASSETS ALREADY IN SERVICE

This segment of the chapter deals with the situation discussed in ASC 360-35-22 (aforementioned), which covers the lives and future depreciation charges for assets already on the books but not yet fully depreciated.

A very simple example, one that in fact requires good internal controls, is the situation of an acquired trade name. Many companies plan to continue to use the trade name they acquired in a business combination. The rules permit trade names to be assigned an indefinite life, which results in no annual amortization charges but does require annual impairment testing. The test, of course, is to determine the fair value of the trade name or brand as of the annual testing date.

What frequently happens is that soon after buying a brand, as part of the total acquisition, the company decides to downplay the acquired brand and concentrate marketing resources on its existing brands. What then happens is that without continued marketing support, the fair value of the acquired brand starts to decline, resulting in an unfortunate impairment charge.

If the brand had been assigned a long but finite life, say 30 years, there would have to be annual amortization charges of just over 3% a year of whatever amount was assigned to the brand. But once a definite life has been assigned, the impairment test changes.

In this case the company first has to determine the current fair value of the asset (brand name in this example). Then an impairment charge is taken, assuming the current fair value is below the amount originally assigned. Finally, a new and definite life is assigned and amortization commences from that point forward. Subsequent annual impairment testing is then done on the brand name on an undiscounted cash flow basis. As long as there are still some sales of product under the acquired trade name the chances are very good that there will be no further impairment charges.

If, however, the company did not change the life, and kept it at indefinite, then it is likely that the fair value would decline year by year and it would be necessary to have repeated impairment charges. Shareholders and creditors can understand a single impairment charge, one year, because nobody and no company bats 1.000. But repeated impairment charges in succeeding years for the *same* asset will lead to embarrassing questions.

TESTING FOR GOODWILL

At this point we have looked at two of the three separate impairment tests called for in GAAP. Remember, these tests should be performed in the following order:

1. Testing the Fair Value of Intangible—Assets that are *not* being amortized (Topic 350).
2. Testing of Property, Plant, and Equipment, and using the same methodology testing of intangible assets that are being amortized (Topic 360).
3. Testing of Goodwill.

It is now time for the most difficult, and often most painful. The American Institute of Certified Public Accountants (AICPA) is developing a practice aid on impairment that might be available at the time this chapter is being read. The practice aid goes into a lot more detail than we can possibly cover in this chapter, and for answers to very specific questions the practice aid[1] will be a very good source.

The following are the required steps, and each of them is discussed in order:

Step 1. Determine Reporting Units
Step 2. See if Reporting Unit has goodwill

Step 3. If no goodwill is present in a Reporting Unit, go on to the next Reporting Unit

Step 4. If the Reporting Unit has goodwill, then determine the fair value of the Reporting Unit

Step 5. If the fair value of the Reporting Unit is equal to or greater than the book value of the Reporting Unit, by definition there is no impairment and you stop

Step 6. If the fair value is *less* than the carrying amount or book value, you then must go to Phase II

Step 7. Phase II is equivalent to a full-scale allocation of purchase price, to be performed in accordance with the rules of ASC 805, using the fair value (as determined in Step 4 as equivalent to the purchase price)

Step 8. Add up the new fair values of all the identifiable assets in the Reporting Unit, subtract the sum from the fair value of the Reporting Unit

Step 9. The difference is now the new "implied" goodwill, which is then compared to the actual goodwill. If the old goodwill on the books is higher than the new implied goodwill, you must write the goodwill on the books down to the new level, resulting in an impairment charge

 ## REPORTING UNITS

In developing ASC 350 which covers impairment testing (formerly SFAS 142) the FASB developed a new concept, called a Reporting Unit. The definition given is:

> "The level of reporting at which goodwill is tested for impairment. A Reporting Unit is an operating segment or one level below an operating segment (also known as a component)."

After reading the above definition a couple of times, it may still not be clear what they are getting at. What it boils down to is that a reporting unit is the same as a segment of the business for which the company has to report sales, operating profit, assets, and so forth. Or, if the segment itself has lower-level businesses for which complete financial statements are available, then that lower-level unit is considered a reporting unit.

The importance of the reporting unit lies in the fact that the company, or its valuation specialist, must determine the fair value of that unit on the impairment testing date, which has to be at the same point each year (e.g., at the end of the third quarter). Thus, to be able to determine the fair value, it is necessary that financial information must be available that is comparable in scope to financial statements issued by publicly traded companies. As noted previously, if a reporting unit does not have goodwill, you do not have to determine its fair value. By the same token, if it does have goodwill on its balance sheet, you must determine the fair value of the reporting unit.

DETERMINING THE FAIR VALUE OF A REPORTING UNIT

The easiest way to develop the fair value of a small publicly traded business is to look at the latest stock price, and multiply it by the number of outstanding shares. This gives what is known as the market capitalization. If you add to that amount the outstanding debt (not current liabilities, but bank debt and other long-term interest-bearing obligations), you have the business enterprise value (BEV).

The rule is that in Phase I you first have to compare the fair value of the unit to its carrying amount. If the fair value is greater than the carrying amount, you stop. By definition there is no impairment. Only if the fair value is less than the carrying amount do you go to Phase II; this involves essentially a revaluation of all assets in the reporting unit at today's fair value.

To meet the Phase I of ASC 805, the market capitalization (fair value of common stock alone) has to be greater than the book value of the equity. If it is larger, one stops because the company has passed the test and by definition in GAAP there is no impairment of goodwill. Under current rules, the test should probably be done at the equity level, not the BEV level (which includes outstanding debt).

It is obvious that this test, for a publicly traded company, is totally dependent on the current market price of the stock, in relation to the book value, defined as the dollar amount of equity on the balance sheet. In 2008–2009, when the market reached new lows not seen for many years, a large number of companies had to take impairment charges for goodwill, no matter how loudly they argued that "the current [low] price of our stock is only temporary" or "the current price of our stock does not reflect our value" or "our Board believes the current price of our stock is way underpriced."

As it turned out, of course, all of the above three arguments were correct. Stock prices rebounded. Unfortunately, under GAAP, once an impairment charge is taken it cannot subsequently be reversed no matter how well the stock price behaves. Interestingly, under IFRS, such reversals are sometimes possible.

But how do we perform the test for a reporting unit of a company which by itself is not traded publicly, or for any privately held company with no stock price that can be looked up in *The Wall Street Journal*? This becomes the domain of valuation specialists (the author in the light of full disclosure does perform this task).

Inasmuch as entire books have been written as to how to value a business, we can only outline here what appraisers do, not tell readers enough for them to "do-it-yourself."

Appraisers generally value businesses, or units of a larger business, using two separate and distinct methodologies. The first is a discounted cash flow (DCF) approach and the second is often referred to as a market comparable approach. A DCF analysis relies on projections of future operating results, while the market comparable approach looks at what other "comparable" companies actually trade at in the market.

When companies are afraid they may not pass Phase I, and want to avoid an impairment charge, we often see very optimistic sales and profit forecasts. The reason is clear, if the company predicts great cash flows over the next five years, the present value of the company will be high. And if the present value is high the company passes the test! No wonder company managements sometimes appear to be extremely optimistic.

From the perspective of an independent appraiser, and the company's own auditors, it is hard to argue with an optimistic forecast prepared by management, even if there is a suspicion that the optimism is really based on a desire to avoid impairment. All that can be said, in effect, to that management is "Well, you are pretty optimistic, and we hope you make it. But if you do not achieve these projections, then next year we will have to scrutinize your projections much more closely." Sometimes companies can dodge the impairment bullet for two years with optimistic forecasts that boost the value of the company under a DCF methodology. Inevitably, the third year comes around and the audit firm, fearing the wrath of the Public Company Accounting Oversight Board (PCAOB) and SEC will not accept continuing projections that are not met.

While there is some scope for "judgment" in the DCF approach to valuation, when appraisers use the market comparable method, the client is really going to be at the mercy of the stock market. This is because the prices of the stock of most companies in a particular industry go up and down more or less at the same time. Thus, a privately held chemical company is going to have a much lower value when chemical company stocks are selling at a price-earnings (P/E) level of seven to eight times compared to better times when most of the chemical companies trade at a P/E of 13 to 14 times.

The Phase I test for goodwill impairment effectively values a company at a single point in time, and does not evaluate future trends. Sharp rises and falls in stock prices, up to ten percent or more in a single day, lead many observers to challenge the underlying logic of the FASB approach. But the rules are in place and there is virtually no flexibility in their application, as many companies found out in 2008–2009.

PHASE II TEST OF ACCOUNTING STANDARDS CODIFICATION 350

Remember, the impairment testing required by ASC 350 is truly binary. You either pass the test and then immediately stop, or you fail the test. In that case you must to go the next step, referred to as Phase II. Phase II is far from trivial, or inexpensive. Essentially, the valuation specialist (auditors usually preclude a client from doing this itself) performs a complete purchase price allocation, using the new BEV as equivalent to a purchase price.

The surprise result is often that there will be identifiable intangible assets in the reporting unit that had never been recognized before on the balance sheet. So if an acquisition were originally placed in a reporting unit that had several valuable trade names, the values of those trade names would *not* be on the balance sheet since companies cannot capitalize self-developed intangibles. If the reporting unit flunks Phase I, then in the process of performing Phase II the appraiser must value *all* of the brand names, customer relationships, and so forth including those for which values had never been developed. These values are all added up and compared with the BEV. The *difference* between the BEV and the sum of the values is called implied goodwill by the FASB.

The difference between the implied goodwill and the recorded goodwill then is the amount of the impairment charge. In other words, the dollar amount of goodwill now to be on the books is the amount calculated as shown previously and which we called the implied goodwill. It must be emphasized that the values of the trade names not recognized before do not get added to the balance sheet. Any new determinations of fair value for any of the assets as determined in Phase II (either more or less than shown on the books) cannot, and do not get reflected on the books. The exercise is carried out for one purpose, and one purpose only, to calculate the implied goodwill. All the other work remains on the working papers and is never reflected on the books of account.

This sounds like a lot of work and it is. A different, but equally good, answer could have been derived by comparing the new BEV with the book value of the reporting unit and simply subtracting that amount from recorded goodwill. We have no idea why the FASB developed such an elaborate requirement, particularly since you cannot take advantage of all the work you have done to develop fair values for all the assets in the reporting unit; put a different way, the company receives no benefit or credit for the increase in value not shown on the existing balance sheet.

The lesson to be learned from this exercise is simple and straightforward, if sometimes difficult to apply in practice. Any time a company overpays for an acquisition it is setting itself up for a future impairment charge. *The only way to avoid this is if the acquisition is placed in a reporting unit that is very profitable and for which there is little likelihood of its ever failing the Phase I test.* In that situation an overpayment will be buried forever.

Our recommendation, therefore, is that whenever possible new acquisitions should be placed in existing reporting units. Setting up the new business as a separate reporting unit is almost guaranteed to produce a future goodwill impairment charge if the buyer paid too much. Since statistics suggest that 70% of acquisitions do not work out, placing one in an existing profitable reporting unit may at least preclude a subsequent impairment charge. Of course avoiding an impairment charge does not turn a bad acquisition (over-payment) into a successful acquisition.

 ## UNDERSTANDING IMPAIRMENT CHARGES

Many companies try to "spin" the situation when they are forced to take an impairment charge. The explanation when impairments of PP&E or goodwill are taken that "this is a noncash charge" has the unstated implication that noncash charges are immaterial.

Of course when the assets were originally acquired, for cash, nobody said "We just spent cash on this asset" because the outlay was capitalized and did not hit the profit and loss statement (P&L) immediately. The author usually takes with several grains of salt managements who brush off impairment with the noncash charge explanation. The fact remains, there was an original cash outlay and at least from today's perspective part of that cash outlay was wasted!

In fairness, nobody can foretell the future. Things do not turn out the way they were expected and every reader has had several instances where hindsight suggested that an earlier investment probably was not a good idea. We cannot be paralyzed out of fear of making a mistake. Some investments will turn out better than expected, and others will go down as a "good try."

The complaint here is the assumption that impairment charges do not matter. They do matter because they are a bright light shining on *prior* decision making.

Particularly in the area of business combinations, where statistics show that perhaps only 30 to 40% of deals are successful, we see a lot of impairment charges. As valuation specialists we are asked to allocate purchase price of a business combination in accordance with ASC 805 (previously SFAS 141 (r)). Part of our analysis is to look at the projections used in justifying the purchase, compare the projections with the purchase price, and calculate an internal rate of return (IRR).

Often we find very low IRR which is an indication that perhaps our client, the acquirer, overpaid for the acquisition. When two or three years later the company has to take an impairment charge to write down—or even totally write off—the goodwill, the message should be crystal clear: "Things did not work out the way we anticipated. With hindsight we made a mistake and overpaid."

Instead, the company's public relations gurus put a "spin" on the situation and imply (perhaps not in so many words) "We were simply a victim of circum-stances. Anyone else in the same situation would have done the same thing."

From our perspective, an impairment charge is recognition of a past mistake. Admit it, and go on. Do not pretend that noncash charges do not matter. They do matter because cash spent on a bad acquisition, or an overpayment for a good acquisition, is gone forever.

Mistakes will continue to be made. Just do not pretend that they are irrelevant.

 ## SUMMARY

Any time actual operating losses occur unexpectedly, or the future outlook calls for operating losses, specific impairment tests should be made, if for no other reason than to demonstrate that internal controls are effective.

Experience with impairment testing also shows that there are relatively few impairment charges associated with PP&E. Intangible assets acquired in a business combination often must be adjusted downward, related in large part to the fact that many mergers involve excessive payments by the buyer. But for PP&E, acquired in the normal course of business and being used for the purpose for which they were originally acquired, impairment charges are rare.

On the other side of the ledger, goodwill impairment charges are fairly frequent, representing one of two situations:

1. Initial overpayment
2. Subsequent adverse economic conditions

The FASB instituted the *un*discounted future cash flow test in order to minimize such impairment charges, and they succeeded. Because the estimation of future cash flows associated with a group of operating assets involves significant management judgment, both of sales, and of costs, in addition it is safe to say that the only actual charges occur when management is willing to take the hit. Not surprisingly, when the outlook is bleak, and shareholders and creditors know this, an impairment charge is often disregarded by analysts. At the same time, following the charge, future operations will not be burdened with as high depreciation charges.

But goodwill impairment charges are quite different and should be viewed by management, boards, and analysts as recognition of past mistakes. But as the saying goes, "mistakes happen."

 NOTE

1. The author was a member of the Task Force, which developed the practice aid.

CHAPTER SIX

Physical Control of Property, Plant, and Equipment

THERE ARE AT LEAST two essential elements of internal control when we are dealing with Property, Plant, and Equipment (PP&E). One is knowing what you are supposed to have, which is the purpose of the fixed-asset register or master file. The other is being able to locate the actual assets, to provide assurance that the property register represents what is physically present.

As mentioned several times in this book, so-called fixed assets in practice are far from "fixed" physically. It never ceases to amaze those who have taken a physical inventory of PP&E how many items cannot be found where the property record says they should be.

With the possible exception of a 1,000-ton press having a 15-foot concrete foundation, virtually all other pieces of equipment can be moved. And often are moved. Keep in mind that even the largest items were brought into a facility from a supplier and erected or installed there. What moved coming in can still move within a company.

Office furniture and fixtures, including computers and IT assets, are easily moved. Every time there is a corporate reorganization, people, desks, files, and phone equipment, not to mention computers are transferred. These moves are sometimes within the same physical facility or building; at other times people literally move to other locations and take their "stuff" with them.

There is only one way to be absolutely sure that the property register is correct, this is by ensuring that the control totals for PP&E on the general ledger are represented by actual assets where they are recorded as being. This assurance can only be obtained from a physical inventory. Periodic inventories of raw materials, work in process (WIP), and finished goods must be taken at least once a year, and that inventory should be monitored by independent auditors. Product inventories are priced out, reconciled to the books, and the control totals adjusted based on what is owned by the company and found during the physical inventory. The same testing of the controls has *not* usually been performed for PP&E.

Why is the same set of procedures undertaken by most companies for inventories not performed for PP&E? Basically because it is not absolutely mandated by Generally Accepted Auditing Standards (GAAS). In the 2005 edition of *Wiley Practitioner's Guide to GAAS*[1], the only reference to fixed assets is in "Section 326—Evidential Matter," which presents a listing headed "Source List of Procedures or Evidential Matter." Under the heading of Physical Observations of Inventory, related to "existence or occurrence" the authors recommend a "plant tour, looking at documents supporting confirmations and acquisitions," and then a general requirement that auditors review "minutes, representations, and other information regarding management's intention to abandon or dispose of fixed assets."

Following that, the authors then suggest auditors review "Documents supporting acquisitions, including authorizations in minutes, construction contracts, purchase orders, invoices, work orders, and so on." Also required, according to the authors, is "confirmation of fixed assets pledged under loan agreements, and so on." Finally, "Confirmation of equipment maintained at outside locations" is called for.

Then, in a catch-all, it is recommended that auditors should look at "Appraisal reports, replacement cost quotations, and so on; recalculation of depreciation and amortization; analytical relationship of current year's depreciation and amortization to fixed-asset costs; and a review of controls over construction contracts payable, vouching of repair and maintenance expense accounts and review of controls over accounts payable and cash disbursements as well a review of control over construction work in progress."

Nowhere in this 2005 edition is there a reference to any sort of formal audit requirement explicitly to check that the assets on the property register are still there, which is the subject of this chapter. Reviewing approvals for capital expenditures and monitoring payables disbursements represent sound auditing, but our experience, and that of most other valuation specialists dealing in PP&E, is that these audit issues mentioned may be necessary, but they are not sufficient.

Many management letters from auditors to the company recommend year after year that a physical inventory be taken of PP&E. In most instances this recommendation goes to the bottom of management's priority list, and does not get accomplished before the next year's audit. The next year's management letter provides the identical recommendation of taking a physical inventory. This can go on for years.

It is obvious that the auditing focus has been on proper authorizations for acquisition and disposition of fixed assets and correct calculation of expense items. Given the accuracy of modern software, reviewing the depreciation calculations themselves is going to be an exercise in futility. What is important is that the basic records themselves are accurate and nowhere does it seem that auditors must monitor a taking of a physical inventory of PP&E, the way they are required to do for inventory records of raw materials, WIP, and finished goods.

When we come to the current edition of the *Wiley Practitioner's Guide to GAAS—2010*,[2] things are even murkier. Section 326 has been renamed "Audit Evidence" as a result of the issuance of SAS 106. Now in the index to the latest volume there is no entry for fixed assets, neither is there an entry specifically related to PP&E.

Section 326 does require the auditor to challenge management assertions about the existence of assets shown on the balance sheet. Also the valuation of those assets (should there be an impairment charge?) should be challenged, according to the Guide. Nowhere is there an explicit requirement that periodic inventories of fixed assets be taken, compared to the property record and differences reconciled. Yet it is hard to understand how management, as well as independent accountants, can assert the property register is correct without verification from an inventory.

Certainly, our experience with client asset listings suggests that there can be upward of 15% discrepancies. For almost any company, an error of ±15% of PP&E would have to be deemed "material." We predict that as more experience is gained with Sarbanes-Oxley (SOX), and as other systems are improved it is only a matter of time that proper attention will be given to inventory and reconciliation of fixed assets.

TAGGING OF PROPERTY, PLANT, AND EQUIPMENT

It would be difficult, with only a description of an asset, to go from the detailed asset listing on a computer and try to find a specific asset on the floor. Take desks, for example, where there are rarely serial numbers, as there are on machine tools. You could take a listing for a Cincinnati milling machine that incorporated the serial number and model number and put your finger on that exact machine, assuming it had not been moved, transferred, or traded in. But could you do that for a "Desk – Wood" or "File Cabinet – 4 drawer," or a "Dell – 19-inch Computer Monitor?" While the monitor may have a serial number, it could be hard to distinguish one from another.

Asking the question provides its own answer. Some easy means of identifying specific items is necessary. Most companies tag assets as they are acquired. This tag number is physically attached to the asset itself. The tag number then becomes the primary identifier in the property record. So, if you want to find out about a particular machine tool, entering the tag number (sometimes called the asset number) into the master property file will bring up the complete record. A moment's thought will confirm that this is essentially the only approach that will work when trying to find a specific asset in a file that may have thousands of items.

The tag should be physically placed on the asset at the time it is received. Some one individual, or department, has to be tasked with this responsibility. It is totally unrealistic to expect someone in the accounting department to run down to the receiving dock every time you receive an item classified as having to be capitalized. Exhibit 6.1 is an example of such a tag, which has detachable labels that can be placed on the appropriate paperwork, showing that the tag was attached, and that the tag number is for that specific asset. Further, since the tags come in prenumbered, this can provide a numerical control for purposes of further internal control.

EXHIBIT 6.1 Property Tag Example

The tags are usually ordered from a source that specializes in this specific function, and below we discuss the alternatives available. The tags will be received preprinted, each with a unique number. After the tag is affixed to the physical asset, a document must be prepared that sends the information to the property accountant; alternatively with appropriate software the information could be transmitted automatically. Since most items will have a purchase order (P.O.), it should be sufficient for the receiving department to reference the tag number, a brief description of the asset, its manufacturer's serial number, and the P.O. The property accountant can then go to the P.O. file, or the capital expenditure (capex) control file, and obtain all of the information needed to add to the master record.

Consider when an item previously capitalized, one already in the master file, is disposed of; all that is necessary is to reference the asset or tag number which should trigger accounting entries. The accounting requirements, to record any cash received and reverse out the asset and accumulated depreciation, should immediately follow the physical disposition. Important as it is, this notification is even more important on a trade-in. There will have been no cash receipts to trigger an entry.

A P.O. will probably reference the existence of a trade-in, or the trade-in may be in the capex approval file; in any event failing to record trade-ins is the primary cause of many errors in internal control. The reverse is also sometimes true. A vendor will offer to accept a trade-in as a means of lowering the purchase price, the company accepts that offer, but the vendor has zero use for the old asset and neglects to collect it and take it off the premises. Then what happens is that accounting records will reflect this assumption that the trade-in physically has taken place, when in reality the old asset is still there. The company may well have written the old asset off the books, and stopped calculating depreciation expense. But, of course, the asset is still there and available for use.

Again, this practice, of a vendor not removing a trade-in, is one of the many causes for discrepancies between the file and the floor. There is no easy or good solution for this other than monitoring by internal auditing that corporate fixed-asset policies are being followed. This is not to suggest that a company should *force* a vendor to take the asset. It does mean that a potential uncertainty should be resolved one way or the other.

 ## ALTERNATIVE TAGGING METHODS

It is almost impossible to have effective internal control over PP&E unless the company assigns individual unique identifying numbers to each asset that will be capitalized. This asset number, physically attached to the item and associated with the master property record file, is the basis of all subsequent internal control. There are essentially two separate types of asset tags, and we discuss each: (1) Barcode and (2) RFID (radio frequency identification).

There is, theoretically, a third which would be a simple numerical label without a barcode. Actually, a barcode tag is nothing but a "numerical" label, where the number on the tag is represented by a barcode font, and usually by a human readable font as well. There is really no difference between the tags, it is just a matter of making data entry faster and more accurate by using a barcode, and a barcode reader for data entry, rather than a human typing on a keyboard. Inasmuch as the cost of maintaining good internal control over fixed assets is substantial, considering periodic physical inventories and subsequent reconciliation, while going for the absolute lowest cost approach makes little sense. Rather, the choice between barcode and RFID should be made on a Total Cost of Ownership basis.

BARCODE TAGGING

It would be difficult for the initial out-of-pocket costs for a barcode system to exceed $3,500. Buying a top-of-the-line barcode label printer might cost $500 to $600, while an equal quality barcode reader could be $700 to $800 and supplies would not exceed $100 to $200. And good quality printers and readers are on the market for far less. This presumes a do-it-yourself approach, although we recommend purchasing pre-printed tags. The cost is truly miniscule when compared to the total costs of internal control.

The "do-it-yourself" tags, especially in that price range, are generally inkjet on paper or thermal resin on paper solutions. They are not the thermal resin on polyester, security polyester, laminated polyester, security reflective vinyl, Lexan Laminated polyester, or metal tags that most asset tag companies offer. In terms of durability (both indoor and outdoor, and in extreme environments), and chemical resistance, there is no comparison. Do-it-yourself solutions are only appropriate for very light duty applications, where the tag itself will not even be handled by anyone once it is applied.

A quick refresher: Barcodes are what we see on consumer-goods packages. They are the funny lines on the box that goes through a scanner at a supermarket checkout counter. The printer has coded the label with an item number, and the scanner is hooked up to a computer that looks up the product number and prints out the unit price. Alternatively, at the meat counter a local printer picks up the description, the weight per pound, the number of pounds, and calculates a total price which is then printed out and subsequently read by the scanner at the checkout counter.

For fixed assets the barcode label would have on the tag the consecutive serial number previously assigned to the asset. This asset number is associated, on the master property asset register, with all the relevant information maintained on that asset in the master file, not on the asset tag.

In taking a physical inventory, the auditor or analyst would point the barcode reader at the barcode label previously affixed to the asset. The reader sends out a beam, often a laser, which hits the barcode and the asset number is transmitted back to the reader.

The reader can either store the asset number, to be downloaded later, or there can be a wireless Bluetooth connection to the computer holding the master file. This transmission would then check-off that the asset had been located. Also, if during the process of locating the barcodes on assets, an asset was found *without* a label, this information too would have to be captured, perhaps manually. At the end of the physical inventory, the computer would be set to print out a listing of all the assets that had *not* been located, at which point the reconciliation process would begin.

Barcode labels themselves can be made almost any size and of any material. Considering that many assets are maintained for 30 or more years, and particularly in a factory environment where there is dirt and grease, one should buy the absolute best labels available on the market, labels that are easily seen and read. The adhesive should also be very high quality, because a "lost" barcode label is going to cause significant problems during the reconciliation phase.

Ideally, labels would be affixed to capitalized items as soon as they are received from the vendor; this function should be part of the formal procedures for the receiving department. The purchase order itself should indicate whether an item is to be capitalized and tagged. This way the staff in receiving will know to affix the appropriate tag. Exhibit 6.1 is an illustration of such an asset tag from Mavericklabel.Com. Their web site provides all the information you would need to order the appropriate labels. While costs vary depending on quantity, size, and type of material, you can obtain very good asset tags for between $0.15 and $0.50 each.

The asset tag shown in the exhibit has one significant innovation, a feature that will be very helpful in internal control. Called the **Asset Tracker**® by Mavericklabel.Com there are detachable labels with the asset number. So, when the receiving department physically affixes the tag to an incoming capitalizable asset, the detachable label can be affixed to the receiving report, invoice, or purchase order, thus alerting the property accountant that the asset has been tagged, *and* what the new asset number is.

Many people think that one of the major reasons for having an asset tag is to prevent theft; think of a personal computer, for example. Candidly, no label is going to stop a determined thief, and there is no such thing as a label or tag that cannot be removed. What the asset tag can do is reduce fraud. It is conceivable that a disgruntled employee could buy an inexpensive laptop and transfer the asset number from the company-supplied MacBook Air. He could walk off with the high-priced computer as he quit, and he would leave behind a computer with an appropriate company asset tag on it; it is just that the tag would not match up the actual computer with the original record assuming someone actually checked it. To counter this potential fraud, some asset tags can be ordered that pop up with the word "VOID" if one attempts to remove the tag from the asset, or which tear into little pieces if one tries to remove it. Either one makes the tag effectively impossible to transfer from one asset to another.

For noncapitalized assets, such as computers, such "VOID" labels might be a very good investment.

The principal disadvantage of barcode tags is that they can get dirty and hard to read, as well as hard to locate. This is particularly true in a manu- facturing environment, but also in a process facility (brewery or refinery) where just what has been tagged in prior years may not be clear from a visual examination. Barcode labels, to be read, must be in direct line of sight.

The one thing you want to avoid if possible is to try and take a physical inventory from a printout of the property record showing the assumed location to be on the floor or in the department you are inventorying. Far better to see the tag visually, record it with the reader, have the computer match up what you found, and print out an exception listing.

RADIO FREQUENCY IDENTIFICATION TAGS

RFID is a far superior way to tag assets. With RFID, you do not have to have direct line of sight; your reader need only be within say three to four feet of the tag.

The one negative to the use of RFID for controlling PP&E cited by suppliers is cost. RFID tags can cost an order of magnitude more per tag than a barcode label and may require some significant system integration efforts through the IT department. As a prediction, in a few years virtually all asset tagging will be with RFID, but we are not there yet.

Let us look at the subject of cost a little more closely. Some studies have suggested it can cost upward of $4 to $5 per year per item, or even more, to maintain the property record. This cost may be exaggerated because of the way the cost calculation is made. Companies are asked how many items are in the property register. Then they take the total cost of the finance department, or controller's organization, and split it among the dozen or so functional activities in the typical company. So total costs for the department are then split among the functions such as:

- Monthly closing
- Accounts payable
- Accounts receivable
- Cash reconciliation
- Budget
- Fixed-asset record keeping

Taking the fully allocated cost for the property system, and dividing by the actual number of items in the register usually will, most likely, produce a high number for the "cost per asset maintained." BUT, these are averages, and certainly do not represent what it costs the company to add one more, or subtract one less, asset from the record-keeping system. So let us cut the average cost more than in half; that still leaves over $1.00 per item per year, just for the accounting function related to PP&E.

Remember, this cost is a yearly cost, and the typical asset has between a five- and 15-year life. That still could come out over the lifetime of an asset to a minimum of $10 per asset item just for record keeping.

Now look at the cost of an RFID tag, maybe $1.50 per item versus $.40 to attach a barcode tag. Yes, the RFID may cost four to five times as much, in percentage terms, but in absolute dollars the net incremental cost of the RFID is little more than a dollar, significantly less than 10% of the lifetime record-keeping cost.

But why incur *any* incremental cost? If, in practice, the barcode tag and the RFID tag produced the *same* results, it would not be worthwhile. The RFID tag has one great advantage, however. All other things being equal, it will significantly *reduce* the time required to take a physical inventory of PP&E. This is because of the way the RFID tag works.

The reader for RFID differs from the barcode reader in one significant way. The beam from the barcode reader must be directly aimed at the tag. So, if the machine with the asset tag attached has been moved and the tag is no longer in sight, then the inventory analyst must hunt for the tag, perhaps go behind the machine to spot the tag and "zap" it. In the worst case, the tag cannot be seen or located and this item now becomes an exception that has to be reconciled and a new tag assigned.

The RFID reader is different. It sends out radio waves, which are picked up on the antenna within the tag, and a response is sent, passively, by the tag to the reader. Now the sensitivity of the reader can be an issue. The reader probably has to be fairly close to the tag, within a few feet, to cause a response. But the tag does not have to be visible to the eye to obtain a hit. Thus, the inventory analyst, carrying an RFID reader, need only be close to the tag and the item will be identified.

If you think about the cost of taking a periodic physical inventory, and the work involved, which would you prefer? The barcode that must be physically seen, or the RFID tag which need only be close to the reader even if it is not visible? It is hard to generalize how much time is going to be saved in taking an inventory with RFID tags, rather than barcode tags. It is hard to imagine, however, that the RFID tag system could take more time.

When you consider the relatively high hourly rate of people taking a fixed-asset inventory, not to mention subsequent reconciliation efforts, it takes very little time reduction to fully justify the initial expenditure on the RFID system. This of course assumes that the company has adopted a relatively high minimum capitalization threshold; this minimizes the number of assets that must be located and accounted for, thus making the higher initial unit cost virtually *de minimis*.

There are a couple of caveats, however, before going down the RFID path. Initial capital expense for implementing a system may be substantially more. It is not just the cost of the RFID labels. Readers can run into the multi-thousands of dollars, while barcode readers can be less than $100. It gets even more expensive if you want a real-time system that monitors all floors and rooms of your facilities, so you can locate an asset without having to do an inventory. That, however, would most likely be a second-step in a program of internal control for fixed assets.

RFID installations generally require an integrator to work with the customer onsite for initial needs assessment and installation. Otherwise, the customer may be buying a whole lot of incompatible hardware.

Another aspect of RFID asset management that is often overlooked is that without individual discipline, it is much more open to the fraud problem that VOID asset tags or destructible vinyl asset tags are designed to prevent. If the inventory procedure does not include actually verifying the tag on the asset, then fraud might be possible and the perpetrator go absolutely undetected.

All one would have to do is take the RFID asset tag off the asset, and leave it somewhere near where the asset was, and where it would be when an inventory is done. If the inventory person does not actually physically verify the asset, they will see the response from the RFID asset tag, and assume everything is okay. In reality, though, instead of a valuable asset, all the company would have is a worthless RFID tag!

ASSET TAGGING FOR EXPENSED ASSETS

Just as there is no necessary connection between lives and depreciation methods chosen for books and taxes, there is no necessary connection between expensing of an asset and attachment of an identification tag. In brief, it is both possible, and often necessary, for a company to identify its property, even if the original acquisition had been charged to expense rather than set up as a capital asset.

Particularly for IT equipment such as personal computers, cell phones, and other small portable items, companies must attempt to control these assets. If a business has a very good, functional, property control system, it should be used for *all* corporate assets, particularly those that might "wander off" if an employee quits.

This means that a property tag can be affixed to a computer or other mobile device, and the tag number and asset description recorded in either the main property system, or in an "off-line" system specifically set up for expensed items.

In other words, the decision whether to charge an item to expense, or to capitalize it, can and should be made irrespective of whether a property identification tag is on the asset or not. Elsewhere we recommended a relatively high minimum threshold for capitalization, perhaps $5,000 per unit. The purpose or objective is to minimize the number of assets the company must reconcile if it is to meet the requirements of good internal control. It certainly is easier to control or look after 2,000 items than 10,000 items, particularly when you should be taking a periodic physical inventory.

But having a high cut-off does not mean you throw caution to the wind and disregard valuable equipment, simply because the initial cost of the item is below the capitalization level set by corporate policy. Many companies put the responsibility for mobile equipment in the hands of Human Resources (when people quit they have to turn in their equipment) or in IT (where assets, including software, can be controlled and upgraded as necessary).

Internal control, in short, does not start and stop with capitalization policies. However, what has been capitalized, and appears as an asset on the firm's balance sheet, does have to be reconciled periodically. Expensed items do not *have* to be inventoried to comply with SOX, although good practice suggests that a periodic check-up is a good idea. Having a property record for capitalized assets, however, that is not representative of total corporate assets is *prima facie* evidence that certain key elements of internal control are missing.

Keeping track of valuable assets, whether or not written off initially to expense, is also an important part of internal control. Neither internal auditors nor independent accountants (outside auditors) usually monitor or report on expensed items. This is probably the reason that companies use low capitalization limits, just to be sure that attention is paid to low-cost but nonetheless valuable assets. But, as discussed in Chapter 2, if the property file is too large, it becomes overwhelming to carry out a complete physical inventory.

Based on the discussion in the previous section of barcode versus RFID tags, for expensed items a barcode label is undoubtedly going to be sufficient. It should be easy to locate a barcode tag on a cell phone or personal computer, and the only issue is making sure that the label material itself, the adhesive, and the printing on the barcode label will withstand constant handling.

 ## RECOMMENDATION

Irrespective of the company's capitalization policies, all assets that have continuing value, and are likely to be "lost," such as personal computers and cell phones, should be tagged with the company's name and an identifying serial number recorded. Two separate property record files can be maintained. The first, and most important, is the property record for all assets that are capitalized. It is the information in this file that will generate periodic depreciation expense and must periodically be tied out to the financial statements. This is what SOX requires, the periodic checking of the asset file to what is on hand.

The second file, of items charged to expense when acquired, can be used by internal managers to help evaluate current and projected expenditures, monitor usage, retrieve assets from departed employees, and generally minimize risk. IT departments have to know what hardware is hooked up to the company network, both for control and productivity. Paying for software by the number of actual users requires accurate information, as does the understanding of projected replacement for both hardware and software.

Essentially there are different uses for these two files, even though on the surface they both deal with company-owned "assets." Trying to put all this data in one large massive file actually works against the goal of true internal control. For this reason we strongly recommend maintaining two separate systems, although the same software can be used for both systems.

The true property record represents the assets that are on the balance sheet, assets which must be accounted for to meet the SOX requirement. The second file is a management tool that may increase productivity and reduce costs.

These two files have certain similarities, but trying to combine them in one overall system will actually be counterproductive.

SUMMARY

In this chapter we provide an outline for physical control of PP&E. Asset tags should be affixed to all incoming items that will be capitalized. A separate series of tags can be applied to expense items of high value such as cell phones and personal computers

There are two basic types of asset tags: barcode and RFID. Barcode tags are much less expensive initially. In taking a physical inventory of PP&E it may be difficult to locate the tag, which then involves research time to reconcile. The advantage is that the inventory analyst does have to look at the asset and make sure it is as described in the property ledger. You want to avoid having the tag on an expensive asset moved by an employee to a similar but less expensive asset.

RFID tags are substantially more expensive when you include any necessary software integration. Once the system is set up, RFID will significantly reduce the amount of time required to take the type of physical inventory we believe is required by SOX.

NOTES

1. Dan M. Guy, D.R. Carmichael, and Linda A. Lach, *Wiley Practitioner's Guide to GAAS: Covering All SASs, SSAEs, SSARSs, and Interpretations—2005* (New York, NY: John Wiley & Sons, 2005).
2. Steven M. Bragg, *Wiley Practitioner's Guide to GAAS: Covering All SASs, SSAEs, SSARSs, and Interpretations—2010* (New York, NY: John Wiley & Sons, 2010).

CHAPTER SEVEN

Taking a Physical Inventory

A CRITICAL ELEMENT IN any system of internal control is verification that what the control totals say actually represents the underlying reality. Are receivables really owed to the company? Send out a confirmation. Does the company really have the finished goods inventory as per the balance sheet? An annual physical inventory, priced out and then reviewed by the external auditors is considered to provide positive evidence that the books of account properly reflect the current inventory situation.

As discussed earlier in the book, a periodic physical inventory of Property, Plant, and Equipment (PP&E) is essential, albeit not directly or explicitly required by generally accepted auditing standards (GAAS) or the Public Company Accounting Oversight Board's (PCAOB's) Statement 5, "An Audit of Internal Control Over Financial Reporting That Is Integrated with an Audit of Financial Statements." It seems to be only a matter of time, however, before internal control over fixed assets does require a periodic inventory and reconciliation.

There are two major potential problems that an inventory will uncover. The first is the existence, actually the nonexistence, of assets on the books. By popular reckoning these are usually referred to as "Ghost Assets," as in they should be there but we cannot find them. For the second, the author coined the term "Zombie Assets," which describes those assets actually present physically, but that do not appear on the asset register or listing.

The reason that it is important to take an inventory of PP&E, and then reconcile it to the books, is that more often than not such an inventory will reveal significant discrepancies; to use a more descriptive term the inventory will reveal errors in the property record. These errors should be corrected in order to properly report on property tax filings, cover owned assets for no more insurance than necessary, and drop from coverage assets no longer there. Finally, almost self-evident, a correct property register that matches actual assets owned will provide correct and supportable periodic depreciation calculations.

Current fixed-asset software will very quickly calculate current depreciation expense, virtually as fast as you can hit "enter" on your computer. But the resultant dollar amount is no more reliable than the contents of the underlying property record. Experience teaches that for many companies, taking a physical inventory of PP&E might reveal an error rate approaching 15%, partially offset by zombie assets not recorded on the books.

 ## PLANNING AND USING THE PHYSICAL INVENTORY

Taking a physical inventory of PP&E is absolutely not a trivial exercise. Properly planned and executed you will find that the first effort is going to be more trouble than you ever imagined. Offsetting this is that once reconciled, taking a subsequent inventory will actually be virtually routine.

The organization of the inventory has to be the primary task of one individual, or a small group of individuals. The people doing the actual work will require management support, because operating managers in other departments are not going to want to divert time away from current work to "some sort of accounting that will accomplish nothing for me."

The following list of questions should be thoroughly reviewed, and plans drawn based on the answers. Below, each of the issues is discussed and suggestions made.

- Who will be responsible?
- Use own staff or outsource?
- Start with current minimum cutoff or go to higher cutoff?
- One floor/department/building at a time or entire company at once?
- Go from present record to assets, or go from assets to record?

- How will you handle the reconciliation?
  - How much effort should be put in?
  - Try to offset ghost assets with zombie assets?
- What to do with fully depreciated assets?
- Do you set up new (revised) asset lives?
- Will the information be used for updating insurance?
- Will the information be used to update property tax assessments?

These are probably the major questions that have to be answered before you actually start taking an inventory of PP&E. We go over them one by one, with our recommendations. But what is important is that the inventory be taken and reconciled, not that these points be followed precisely.

One word of warning. Taking and reconciling a complete inventory is not a trivial exercise. It is going to be time consuming and costly. As my wife once told me in regard to a home-improvement project, "We should count on it taking twice as long and costing three times as much as we expect, unless it takes three times as long and only costs twice as much as we expect." Of course, when the project was completed, and we looked at each other, the correct answer was crystal clear: It took three times as long *and* cost three times as much as we originally expected. Fortunately, we were happy with the outcome and soon forgot the pain. Whatever your initial time estimate for a physical inventory of fixed assets, you would be safe in doubling it.

The point is that a cost budget for the project, laid out in terms of time, with recognizable milestones is a necessity. By the time you are finished you may well have busted the budget, both in time and in terms of cost. Nonetheless, at least you have to have some idea of what is going to be involved. No one should simply start counting and hope for the best.

 WHO SHOULD BE RESPONSIBLE?

At the end of the day responsibility should be placed on someone who can get the job done. Candidly, we do not recommend that the property accountant be in charge of the project. This is true for two reasons. First, while there are some exceptions, property accountants have not usually reached a management level, with management experience. Second, just in terms of good internal control, the individual responsible for maintaining the record in the future should not be the one who puts it into initial shape.

There are many fine people who fulfill the role of property accountant in their company. It is an important job that must be done well. However, there is very little glamour or romance in the position. Many ambitious accountants in the company may feel that being in budgeting, cost accounting, or financial reporting will have more visibility and greater promotion possibilities. Property accounting should not be a "dead-end" job, but unfortunately all too often the incumbent acts that way, and it becomes a self-fulfilling prophecy.

It is our recommendation, based on the size of the company, that the internal auditor should have the primary responsibility for the task. In most firms the internal auditor has had exposure to top management and the board of directors. In his or her reports to the Board, and external auditors for that matter, if the internal auditor is in charge of the PP&E inventory and reconciliation, the task will have substantial visibility. Since it is going to be a costly and time-consuming task, you do not want the project to "bog down" and if the Board is looking over the shoulder of the internal auditor that alone will provide the impetus for finishing the job.

There will be some who say that if the internal auditor has been responsible for the file, then how can they then subsequently audit for compliance with company policy the property records that they themselves prepared? The answer is straightforward. Once the record is accurate, then auditing need only see that existing policies are followed. As long as the policies are adhered to, and you have an initial file that you have confidence in, the file can be maintained relatively easily and need not be audited in detail for a long time to come.

What has happened in the past, in most companies, is that nobody really ever checked (or even wanted to check) how good the property records were. The computer software will spit out monthly and quarterly depreciation amounts and people can go on to the next task, irrespective of how inaccurate the records actually are.

Since depreciation is a "noncash charge" many people feel that the absolute dollar amount of depreciation is of little consequence; the accuracy or inaccuracy of the depreciation charges is totally discounted. It is easily assumed that "Something is Better than Nothing"; hence any depreciation charge will do. "We have a depreciation charge that the machine calculated, so it must be correct." If in fact the depreciation charge is incorrect, as we have seen, the implicit assumption is that things will ultimately correct themselves over time, as every asset entry in the system is inexorably written down to zero net book value.

USE OWN STAFF, OR OUTSOURCE?

This question does not have an easy answer. All other things being equal (and they seldom are equal) you would be better off using your own staff. They are familiar with the company, its policies, and most important the right people will themselves be familiar with the assets. IT staff can best inventory computer-related assets; plant engineers are most familiar with the actual machinery on the factory floor; an office manager or office services individual will be most familiar with office furniture and fixtures.

The problem with this approach is that the selected individuals undoubt-edly have other current responsibilities. What will happen to their regular work if they are pulled off for temporary duty on the physical inventory? Unless the overall project has truly top management support (not lip service, but a real desire to have it done in order to comply with Sarbanes-Oxley [SOX]) trying to get key employees from within the company may involve too much effort.

A potentially simpler, albeit perhaps more expensive, solution would be to utilize outside professional help. A company such as Paragon International (www.paragon-net.com) is in the business of putting tags on assets and taking the physical inventory, although they do not do valuation. Valuation firms such as Marshall & Stevens (full disclosure: The author is affiliated with Marshall & Stevens) have a lot of experience in inventories and valuation of all types of assets.

The disadvantage of using outsiders, and the fact that they are not as familiar with the organization, is probably offset by their familiarity with the actual inventory and reconciliation *process*. Your own staff has probably not been involved recently in a physical inventory of PP&E, whereas the outside professionals make their living doing that on a more or less full-time basis. Looking at it objectively the trade-off is knowledge of the company compared to knowledge of how to take and reconcile an inventory.

A good compromise would be to engage outside professionals for the initial effort. Some company personnel will still have to be involved in the inventory and reconciliation process because outside professionals cannot do it all. Those employees who do gain the experience in the initial effort can then handle most of any subsequent inventory reconciliation.

A second inventory, two or three years later, will go much more easily than the initial effort, if only because the property record will have been cleaned up. It probably took 20 or 30 years for the property record to fall behind, and once caught up it will not deteriorate significantly in the first couple of years.

WHAT MINIMUM DOLLAR CUTOFF SHOULD WE USE?

The decision here will have a profound effect, not only on the inventory and reconciliation process, but on future resources to be devoted to the internal control of fixed assets. The reason goes back to our earlier recommendation that companies adopt a relatively high-dollar value for minimum capitalization.

The fewer assets you are trying to control the less effort is going to be required. Nobody tries to "control" the usage of ball point pens. At $.50 or less it would be totally unrealistic to monitor ball point pen usage. Companies have a supplies cabinet and pads of paper, pencils, pens, and so forth are simply there for the taking. Does an occasional pen or pad find its way home for a sixth grader's school requirements? Obviously the answer is yes. Office supplies do get taken for personal use.

Why do companies permit this? The cost of control over ball point pens is going to be greater than the cost of the pens themselves! Most people will not spend $5.00 to save $.50.

At the other end of the spectrum, companies do not have a self-service cabinet for personal computers or smart phones. These are costly items that have great personal appeal; no company can afford to outfit the entire family of every employee with personal computers or BlackBerry Smartphones. Controls are in place as to who gets a computer, what model, and how often it is replaced. Here the cost of control is *less* than the value of the asset(s) involved.

Should this same principle not be applied to control of PP&E? The real risk of office furniture and fixtures, or of production machinery and equipment, "walking off" is quite low. Further, prevention of theft is never going to be accomplished by putting an asset tag on something and recording it in the property ledger. Physical theft requires physical controls (e.g., guards at the door); accounting controls have never been designed for physical control and the two types of control should not be confused.

This brief discussion leads directly to our recommendation. Assume the accounting policy so far has called for capitalization of low dollar amounts, say $500. There is no necessity that you should have to look for, identify, and reconcile such small-dollar items.

If you can locate, identify, and reconcile high-dollar items, then in effect you can disregard the low-dollar items, whether or not they appear on the property register. The Pareto Principle[1] or 80/20 rule applies here. If you can demonstrate good control of 80% of the dollar value of items, it is unlikely that all of the small amounts have vanished. Just disregard them. No auditor is going to insist on a company spending unnecessary resources on small-dollar amount items. Put a different way, had the capitalization policy been higher in the past, and nobody would have complained, why spend today's limited resources to support or reinforce what should not have been done in the first place, that is, trying to control low-dollar value items.

Companies have limited resources. It is far better to put those resources to assure that the majority of the financial statement assets are present and accounted for properly, than to try and control everything and then give up because the task is overwhelming. Companies have got into the present position because taking a physical inventory and reconciling it appears to be a monumental undertaking. And it is, if you really try to locate, identify, and reconcile every item that had been capitalized in the past.

Look at it this way. What has been done has to be accepted. Whatever it is today, is. That does not mean, however, that you have to continue, blindly, accepting that past. You can move on!

The easiest way to move on, therefore, is to inventory and reconcile the 20% of the assets that account for 80% of the dollars. Stop worrying about the large number of small-dollar items, they are not worth spending resources on. The author was involved in a business combination where the target's property records literally included an ashtray ($1.25) and a wastebasket ($2.75), both of which items had been dutifully depreciated annually since acquisition with a ten-year life assigned to each. The buyer really did not care whether or not the ashtray and wastebasket could be found!

While the minimum dollar value limit to be inventoried will differ by company, it certainly would be worthwhile to have the computer sort the property record in descending dollar order. This can be either on original cost or current net book value. Then have the machine cumulate the dollar totals in descending order, and pick the cutoff where 75 to 85% of the dollars are. That can, and should be, the cutoff.

Plan the inventory to find the chosen items, and simply disregard the smaller dollar items. You do not have unlimited resources. Place those limited resources to complete the important part of the inventory and reconciliation. When that has been done, if your heart and mind, or audit firm, tells you to keep going and finish the total job—by trying to get 100% completion—all we can say is Good Luck.

 ## INITIAL EFFORT—PARTIAL FACILITY VERSUS TOTAL

If the company's assets are in a contained geographical area, it would take less total effort to physically inventory everything, and only then go through the reconciliation process. The reason is simple. If you take only a partial inventory, say one floor or one department, you are going to find items that do not appear on the property record for that department. Further, the property record will say that there should be some items that you cannot find.

That is what the reconciliation process is all about. Assume that you start with the property record, which shows the asset number, the description, and the location (floor, department, or building) of the asset. We know, in advance, that the property record is wrong, it is just that we do not know where it is wrong.

Consequently, if you take only one department at a time, you will have missing assets on the one side, and unidentified assets on the other. But what do you do with that information? You cannot write off the ghost items, or write up the zombie assets from a single department. The reason will become clear soon enough. The so-called missing assets in the department you inventoried first actually are in some *other* department. And the zombie assets you found, that are not on this department's printout, really show in the master file as belonging to another department.

In short, the location for assets shown in the property record will not correspond where the assets are. The cause goes back to the lack of control when assets are moved or transferred. The physical move took place, presumably with full management approval, but nobody communicated with the accounting department. How would a property accountant possibly learn about a transfer, unless he or she was told? No property accountant can be expected to wander the halls and aisles every day looking for asset movements. One of the essential elements of internal control, notification to the accounting department regarding asset movements, is usually a missing element if not the key missing element.

With this situation of assets physically being present in areas other than what the property register shows, partial inventories can never be totally reconciled. A ghost asset in one department can never be written off until the total physical inventory is completed. After all if you are 95% done with the first 19 departments (out of 20), the missing asset shown as in Department 1 could be in the yet to be inventoried Department 20. You do not know, and cannot find out, until you are 100% complete.

This in turn suggests that you try to take the entire company, facility, or location at one time, which will minimize the reconciliation effort. But, depending on the size of the company, this total approach could be impractical.

The other problem, if you do the inventory piecemeal, is that while waiting to do subsequent areas there is always the opportunity for an asset to be moved from or into already inventoried areas. Accountants are used to this problem: When inventorying raw materials, work in process (WIP), and finished goods cutoffs *must* be accurate. But since PP&E inventories are so infrequent, the need for cutoffs likely will only appear after a partial inventory has been taken.

The conclusion, and recommendation, is straightforward. If you can do the entire job at one time, all departments, all floors, all buildings, then that is the way to go. If such an approach appears overwhelming, then do each area as quickly as possible, minimizing the chances that inventoried items will be moved elsewhere and counted twice, or an asset not yet counted could be moved to an area where you think you have counted everything.

As discussed in the reconciliation phase (see Reconciliation of the Inventory to the Records section ahead), the question comes if after a partial inventory (one department or one floor) you should try to reconcile each phase, or wait until the end and do a single grand reconciliation. At this point, the answer may be less than straightforward. If the company is relatively small, wait to the end for reconciliation. If the inventory involves multiple locations and thousands of asset listings, the only practical approach may be to do it piecemeal. In the latter case you will end up with one or more unmatched lists, waiting for final resolution until the overall completion.

THE $64,000 QUESTION—ASSETS TO LISTING OR LISTING TO ASSETS?

Actually there are three approaches to taking a physical inventory of PP&E. These are:

1. Print out the current existing property ledger by geographical location (floor, department, etc.), look for the assets that are supposed to be there, identify assets there but not on the printout, and mark on the listing the missing assets. At the end of the project there will be ghost assets and zombie assets that have to be reconciled.
2. Make a listing of the actual assets that are present in a specific area; you then look for them on the existing property record. Those that match are fine, but at the end of the total exercise there will still be ghost assets and zombie assets that have to be reconciled.
3. This approach effectively says the existing property record will cause more trouble than it is worth. Knowledgeable analysts record each asset they find, a true physical inventory, with a description (including serial number)

and an estimate of the condition. Then trained machinery and equipment valuation specialists estimate the fair value of the assets actually on hand. There is no reconciliation, but the sum total dollar amount of the assets on hand undoubtedly will differ from the control totals on the general ledger; a loss may have to be recognized. It is unlikely that auditors would permit the company to "write-up" the total dollar amount of PP&E if there is a gain.

It may be hard to choose between the first two approaches, so one way is to do a test of each approach. Take a department and print out the assets to be found. Then see how many unmatched assets there are, including a brief scan to see if the record of the "missing" assets may be in another department. As a counter, go to a department, list the assets to be inventoried (those in value above whatever minimum was chosen), and see how hard it is to find or identify them in the existing property listing.

When both tests have been completed you probably will decide that one or the other approach will involve less time and effort for your firm. However, if both approaches show up major problems with the existing record there may be little choice but to go to the third approach, a *de novo* inventory, the items on which have to be valued.

As will be discussed in the next section on reconciliation, it is the reconciliation, not the taking of the inventory itself, that takes the most substantial effort and time.

RECONCILIATION OF THE INVENTORY TO THE RECORDS

Regardless of whether the company chooses the first or second approach, starting with the record or starting with the inventory, two things inevitably will happen. First, you can be absolutely certain that many items in the existing property register have not been found during the physical inspection; this of course assumes that assets had previously been tagged and the correct asset tag numbers are in the system. Second, you can be absolutely certain that you will find assets that—for whatever reason—do not seem to be in the existing asset listing or at least you cannot find them.

Consequently, you now have two lists: missing assets and missing listings. In a perfect world without auditors or worrying about internal control, we would: (1) simply estimate the fair value of the assets you found that are not on the listing; (2) subtract the book value of the items on the property listing that cannot be found; and (3) add the value from the first step to the existing listing after the necessary deletions. At that point it would be clear whether there is a net gain or loss. A single entry would be made to bring the control totals in agreement with the new detailed asset listing.

Based on discussions with a number of auditors, none of them seemed willing to approve this "easy way out." The problem was not with writing off the missing assets, but writing *up* the assets you found that do not appear to be accounted for in the existing records and recapitalizing (to coin a new word) the fully depreciated assets still in use.

 ## FULLY DEPRECIATED ASSETS

The reason for disapproving the write-up probably stems from a fear that allowing companies to put assets back on the book that have already been written off is some sort of "double counting." You have already charged the original cost to expense, and writing them up and depreciating them a second time appears to some auditors illogical.

It depends at this point whether one could claim that the too-fast original depreciation of assets, and by definition a fully depreciated asset still in use must have been written off too quickly, is an error, or an incorrect accounting estimate. So how would the analysis go? By definition the original assumed economic life was incorrect and too much depreciation was taken too early. The original estimate of the life was wrong. Is this error—regarding the future time period an asset will be used—an accounting *estimate* that can be corrected or an *error* that would require restatements of all prior years?

If you can convince yourself, and your auditor, that fully depreciated assets still in use simply represent an error in making the original estimate of useful life, you should be able to obtain the current accounting for a change in accounting estimate. Generally accepted accounting principles (GAAP) say that if you correct an accounting estimate, you make the net change in the current year and have it correct from here forward.

To the contrary, correction of a real error requires restatement of all prior years, which publicly traded companies would probably not undertake. A private firm could, at least in theory, be willing to go through a restatement process in order to avoid a writedown from the physical inventory of PP&E coming up short.

How would accountants and auditors react to a fact pattern that says we originally took too short a life, in effect estimating that the economic value would diminish much more quickly than it did in practice?

Some auditors would view reversing that depreciation expense taken over a number of years as a correction of an error and they would require restatement of all prior years. For a privately held company, not subject to Securities and Exchange Commission (SEC) oversight, this might be the way to go. Simply swallow the restatement medicine, take the restatements of prior years and be assured that from here forward there will be good internal control.

Other auditors could be persuaded that all the company is doing is correcting incorrect prior assumptions about future life at the time of the original acquisition. In this scenario the company would be home free.

The advantage of treating the fully depreciated assets as requiring a new and revised estimate is that the gain in the year that the estimate is adjusted is going to go a long way to making the final reconciliation easier for management to accept. Revising fully depreciated assets still in use will offset some of the ghost assets that inevitably exist on today's property register.

Implicit in this discussion is an assumption that most companies will come up short in the initial reconciliation effort. This assumption is based on both our experience and of others who have gone through the complete process. For whatever reason, or reasons, it is hard to find everything that your books of account imply should be there. Assets do not vanish into thin air or evaporate overnight. But, as discussed earlier in Chapter 3, all sorts of things happen. With the passage of time, perhaps 20 years or more, most of the adverse events end up on the short side, not the long side.

 ## RECONCILIATION PROCESS

The starting point should be a listing of assets you found that are not readily apparent on the books. Assets just do not materialize suddenly from the "Dark Matter" in the universe. Someone ordered it, built it, changed it, or otherwise made it difficult to associate with an accounting entry from years past.

Every asset, of any material amount, should be traced back to an accounting entry. The first step has to be to go to the department where the asset is and ask the manager, supervisor, or employee with the longest service, "Where did this come from?" That simple question will, more often than not, get answered in a way that helps the reconciliation team trace it back.

We use the word "team"; the reconciliation process cannot use a lot of people, but it can utilize the time of two or three people, at least one of whom should be from the accounting department. The other team members are dependent on the type of company involved, with computer-based firms requiring IT expertise while a chemical plant certainly needs some engineering expertise.

Some major assets, in dollar value terms that cannot be readily traced back, may well have been modified and/or cannibalized to create a new asset, or built through the use of small-dollar purchase orders so as to get around the firm's capital expenditure approval process. It never ceases to amaze me that managers are permitted often quite high-dollar limits for expenses and very low-dollar limits for capital items. Capital expenditure (capex) policies can be bureaucratic, and slow, and often will have very low-dollar limits. Approval often has to go up much higher than one would like, and busy senior executives may not feel the same sense of urgency as does a production manager struggling to meet a tight quota.

Frustration with "the system" has been known to cause otherwise responsible employees to "bend" the system to meet a short-term goal. Often such efforts are associated with upgrading existing equipment. It should be possible to associate an unmatched physical item with one of the unmatched assets as yet not found in the initial physical inventory, a line on the printout that does not have a checkmark indicating it was located.

Given enough time and effort, most items on hand, those that cannot initially be found in the existing asset register, will be found in the listing under one description or another.

At the end there will be still a few zombie assets. You know you have them, the company owns them, and they simply appear to have mysteriously appeared; this mysterious appearance is the 180° opposite of what is termed "mysterious disappearance" when jewelry cannot be found. There should be relatively few such items. For those few they should be entered into the asset record with an estimated fair value entered into at least the insurable value field. You may not be able to offset this "gain" on your financial statements, but the offset can be used as an explaining feature in the final report to the audit committee, external auditors, and if necessary in a footnote to the financial statements.

After cleaning up the assets physically present, but not initially visible on the existing property register, you will probably still be left with unmatched items, so-called ghost assets. The asset listing shows you paid for them, you supposedly own them, and they simply cannot be found.

This situation, unpleasant as it may be to management, is the purpose of taking the physical inventory to prove the accuracy, or inaccuracy, of the existing property record. The only real choice, after you have come to the conclusion that the ghost assets simply are not there, is to write them off through a charge to expense, which then removes the assets' record from the property register.

The one silver lining to getting rid of ghost assets is that your insurable values should decrease, with a small potential offset in insurance premiums. Also, your filings with the property tax assessing officer should be adjusted, with a proportionate property tax savings. Whether you can go back and claim a refund is a matter of facts and circumstances; it is at least worthwhile to ask the question if you can file amended property tax returns.

While the ghost asset writeoff may be quite large, one way of looking at it is to calculate the number of years since the property record was initially set up. Then divide the number of years into the total dollar amount of the writeoff for missing assets. The amount *per year* will appear much more reasonable. Further, this annual "loss" can persuasively be shown not to recur in the future since we assume you will now have, going forward, a good system of internal control over all fixed assets.

REVISED ASSET LIVES

Once you have analyzed the fully depreciated assets still in use, this will provide solid evidence as to the actual expected life in your business of comparable assets. As noted elsewhere in the book there is no need to use the same lives for books and taxes. You probably will not want to change the tax lives, absent net operating losses that do not provide any benefit for additional depreciation.

But there is no reason to leave existing book lives in place, undisturbed, if you have evidence that the assets will actually provide economic benefits for a much longer period. Remember, depreciation expense is designed to allocate the original cost of the asset over its *useful* life. The useful life for your firm need not necessarily be the same as the useful life for someone else. Therefore, arbitrary rules, or rules of thumb, or simply carrying over tax lives actually is opposite to the intended role of depreciation expense.

A number of years ago inflation was running at a high rate, and the cost of new equipment was substantially higher than the old equipment that had to be replaced. At that time companies were urged to depreciate assets as quickly as possible in order to reflect economic reality. Proposals were made and implemented for a couple of years, of indexing upward the depreciation expense "to provide funds for asset replacement at *current* cost."

The proposal did not work well because (1) companies rarely replace assets on a one-to-one basis; and (2) actual lives were of course longer than the lives being used for financial statements. Indexing of financial statements, favored by the Financial Accounting Standards Board (FASB) and SEC in the late 1970s died a painless death when neither companies nor investors were able to use the new numbers for actual business decisions.

In addition to using information from the fully depreciated asset to review the lives of comparable assets, you are also permitted to use your management judgment on the remaining lives of all PP&E. We do not advocate simply multiplying existing remaining lives by some multiple, say 1.5 times. We do however recommend that as long as you are cleaning up the fixed-asset register this would be a perfect time to review *all* lives.

Today's software, from firms such as Real Asset and Sage, permit you to test out the impact of such changes before you actually change the master file and affect actual depreciation expense permanently. It would seem though that if you have to take a writedown for missing assets you might as well explain that the company has made a total review of *all* aspects of fixed-asset accounting and adjusted remaining lives as needed, with the anticipated changes reducing anticipated depreciation expense for the current year by "X" and for next year by "Y."

SUMMARY

It is highly likely when you take a complete physical inventory of your fixed asset that you will have a net charge to expense. This will be for assets on the books that cannot be found. You may be able to offset this in part by reviewing the depreciation already taken on assets fully written off, but still in use. This category may be more substantial than initially anticipated because the fact is that the economic life of many assets, excluding computer-related IT, is far longer than the usual accounting lives.

Taking a physical inventory is fairly expensive and requires significant resources. You can use your own staff, hire outside specialists, or a combination of both.

Once the inventory has been taken, however, the work is just beginning. Reconciliation of assets present but not accounted for is relatively easy, with enough effort they can probably be tied back to some accounting records.

Assets on the books that you cannot find, ghost assets, do have to be written off, with a charge to expense in the period.

In explanation, you can indicate that you have reviewed the internal controls of PP&E, have brought the records up to date, and have a system in place that will preclude future problems, at least in magnitude comparable to this year's initial write-off or adjustment.

When this reconciliation is complete and all accounting entries have been made, then it should be apparent to everyone that this aspect of internal control called for by SOX has been completed. What if someone asks, "why wasn't this done years ago?" The answer can only be that corporate resources were being devoted to higher priority areas and the time for fixed assets had arrived this year.

 NOTE

1. "The 80/20 rule is probably one of the most powerful ideas which is universally applicable in practically every sphere of our lives. The best part is that it is easy to understand and apply. Yet many people know little about it. The irony is that those who are aware of it, do not use it as often as they should in making decisions." (www.80-20presentationrule.com/whatisrule.html (September 18, 2010).)

8

Reconciliation of Physical Inventory to Accounting Records

I N SOME WAYS THIS may be the most important chapter in the book. We assume that a company recognizes that its internal controls over Property, Plant, and Equipment (PP&E) have to be improved. New policies have been established for minimum capitalization going forward. Asset lives are based on realistic expected lives, not on tax requirements. Acquisition, transfer, and retirement policies will be followed so that the accounting records correspond to the physical assets, and vice versa.

At this point a controller can be satisfied that in the *future* PP&E will be under control. What is missing is the fact that the existing property records, and the actual assets present in the company, are not synchronized. One approach that may have appeal would be to say, "OK we've had problems in the past, but from here forward we undoubtedly will have a good system. Let's just let the old problems sort themselves out over time. After all, every year from now on future-year depreciation charges will bring any past errors closer to resolution. Once all the old assets on our books are written down to zero or to salvage value, we no longer will have a problem. Meanwhile, all the new additions will be controlled, so let's take our limited resources and utilize them elsewhere."

This approach has a certain appeal, and if audit committees and outside auditors were able to live with the former system, and a new and better system is now in place, maybe the company *should* let time heal all the past wounds.

As attractive as this approach might seem, however, there still is one giant problem: Sarbanes-Oxley's (SOX's) requirement for management to certify that a good system of internal control is in place now, not to be in place sometime in the future.

If there can be a significant difference between what the books of account state are today's company assets, and what you believe is there you may have a real problem in currently signing the applicable SOX forms. Is the solution then *not* to take a physical inventory of your PP&E in the first place? Then you would be able to say, "Well, things might be a little off but I don't have any hard evidence as to the magnitude of any potential problem?" Put a different way, is willful ignorance a valid defense? For purposes of this book we do not choose to parse that question.

At this point we assume that the reader, and company management, wants to do the right thing. The right thing, as far as internal control is concerned, is to take the inventory, make the necessary adjustments (even though they may be painful), and be able to certify that the company does, at this point, have internal control over PP&E.

An essential element of any internal control system is correspondence between the records and the underlying assets. A control system for finished goods is checked at least once a year through a physical count or with a perpetual inventory system that has frequent cycle checks. Internal control over cash requires reconciliations of bank statements in order to assert that the banks concur that the company really has the cash that is shown on the balance sheet. Control over accounts receivable is often performed by outside auditors, when they send written confirmation to the firms who the books show still owe for past sales. These three major aspects of current assets (cash, inventory, and receivables) are routinely monitored by internal and external auditors.

Intangible assets and goodwill are now routinely tested for impairment at least once a year, and auditors have been particularly scrupulous in reviewing these tests. At this point there is only one class of assets that is not truly controlled. Seemingly it is only PP&E that is left to its own devices; yet, in many companies more than 20% of total assets are in this category.

Granted, in many management letters auditors will tell the company: "You should take a physical inventory of PP&E and make necessary adjustments." Or the letter will say, "It has been some time since you last reconciled the property ledger and good internal control requires a periodic reconciliation." The problem is that the words in the letter are written to protect the auditor from criticism—"We noticed the problem and brought it to the attention of management, and if they chose not to do anything about it, there's nothing we can do about it!"

That statement, of course, is simply not believable. If the auditors really thought the lack of reconciliation was a critical problem they could state this in their SOX report on internal control, and if they truly believed it was critical they could threaten to withhold the auditor certification. To the best of our knowledge, no auditor has ever gone so far as to refuse to sign an audit report because they felt that there was inadequate control over PP&E. Auditors are accountants, and as mentioned earlier most accountants feel that problems in accounting for PP&E are "self-correcting" in that the sheer passage of time will solve all inaccuracies in property accounting.

TWO APPROACHES TO RECONCILIATION

Assume at this point that either the auditors have put the "fear of God" into the company, or the company itself decides that reconciliation can no longer be put off. How to go about what, in the final analysis, is a significant effort. We believe that there are only two ways that the job can be done so as to ensure the property record really does match the underlying reality of what is out there.

- Method 1 is to take the existing property record, sort it by location, and go out and try to find the assets shown on the listing.
- Method 2 is to go out and take a complete physical inventory of what is out there.
- If Method 2 is chosen then there are two real alternatives:
  - Valuation specialists can price out the assets on hand and that becomes the new property register.
  - One can try and locate on the existing property register the original entries for the assets on hand as shown by the physical listing; then you write off the missing items and write up the assets which are there but not on the register.

To simplify the subsequent discussion let us review two terms which are necessary to understanding and performing this work:

1. Ghost assets (items that are on the books and cannot be located)
2. Zombie assets (items that are physically there, but not on books)

GHOST ASSETS

Our definition of ghost assets is simple: There is an asset listed on the books that cannot be found anywhere in the organization. In short, the asset seemingly is missing, but the dollar amount shown on the balance sheet has never been written off. Thus, at least in theory, the net worth of the company is overstated, at least to the extent of the balance shown for the missing asset.

It is certain that something *not* there fails the Financial Accounting Standards Board (FASB) definition of an asset as "providing future economic benefit that enables it to provide future net cash inflows." Other than the tax benefit from an immediate write-off, or future depreciation charges, it is hard to ascribe value to a true ghost asset. If the financial statements, including the balance sheet, are to faithfully report assets owned by the company, ghost assets must be identified and written off.

Marshall & Stevens has performed several ghost asset engagements for clients, for example, in the retail and gaming industries. Consequently, we have significant experience in just how ghost assets come into being.

The basic or root cause is that as new assets are acquired, the old assets that they replace simply are not written off the books. New slot machines are bought for a casino, since patrons always like to see new opportunities. The old slot machines are moved into a back storage area and forgotten. Then one day the storage area is needed and a supervisor says, "Clear out the old stuff, we'll never use those again."

Whether the old machines are sold, or scrapped, the people involved in physical disposition never give a thought to notifying the accounting department—either when the old assets were moved into storage or when the assets were physically disposed of. Consequently, the property accountant, with no reason to make a change in the records, faithfully continues to report the assets as present and she provides for depreciation expense each year. Without a physical inventory and reconciliation nobody in finance even thinks there is a problem.

In the retail environment, with multiple store locations, fixtures are replaced with new display units, and the old fixtures transferred to other locations or, again, but into a back storage area waiting for something to happen. Inasmuch as old fixtures have relatively little cash value (have you recently tried to sell beat-up display cases?) it is not long before a store manager or supervisor tells a maintenance man, "Get rid of this stuff before we run out of room." Then, the assets are out the door, and again nobody in the central accounting department has the slightest idea of what has happened.

A third example of how ghost assets come to be is a factory expansion. The company wants to expand a 50,000-square-foot warehouse and contracts to add 20,000 square feet of additional space. The original building, built five years ago had cost $3.5 million or $70 per square foot. The contractor quotes $100 per square foot, assuring that the addition will match visually the existing structure. Typically, an addition will cost more per square foot than a brand new building (think of a kitchen remodeling in your own home). The contract is signed, the expansion completed, and the accounting department capitalizes the $2,000,000. Now we have a 70,000-square-foot building on the books with a total original cost of $5.5 million or $78.57 per square foot, which is higher than current construction costs for a new 70,000-square-foot building. In addition to overstating values for property taxes and insurance, the fact is that the company could not sell the warehouse for what it is on the books for, and in a business combination the buyer would determine the fair value to be perhaps less than $5 million since it is actually a five-year-old structure, despite the "new" addition.

Where is the ghost asset here in this very realistic example? Part of the remodeling contractor's quote was the cost for tearing down the outside wall of the original structure, to which the addition will be added. Also, of course, there is the cost to construct the new outside wall. The books of account now reflect two outside walls (only one outside wall exists) plus costs expended to tear down the original wall. The original wall and tear down expense of that wall are now ghost assets, on the books but missing in action. You cannot blame the real estate manager, and there was nothing in the paperwork to suggest what was going to happen and what actually did happen. At the end of the day, the controller, or property accountant, must understand the economics and physical construction of building additions, and make the appropriate accounting entries, in effect not capitalizing the tear down cost and the second wall.

A final example of ghost assets is all too common. The office manager trades in a black and white copier for a new fancy all-in-one color copier, fax, printer, and scanner. Obviously, the new machine will take the place of the existing unit and the salesman says, "If you don't have any use for the machine, we will give you $150 credit and take the machine off your hands." Since the office manager does not want to spend time disposing of the old machine, and probably would not get $150 for it anyhow, he says to the salesman, "Go Ahead." However, the salesman says, "I'll come back later to get the old unit and take it off your hands." If and when he does, the current net book value of the old asset *should* be written off. In many instances this entry is never made, so the books now reflect two units, with only one unit present.

In practice the number of ways items become ghost assets is almost unlimited, but every one of them has one thing in common:

The Accounting Department Was Not Notified!

For all changes affecting PP&E, it is critical that a system be set up so that the accounting department *will* be notified, and the property ledger changed appropriately. Desirable as it might seem to leave the initiative up to the accounting department to find out what has happened, in practice this does not work, unless you have a very inquisitive and very aggressive property accountant—and in many companies property accounting is not given the recognition it deserves.

The company should set up a system whereby each department manager is responsible for the assets in his or her department. If a periodic audit shows assets are missing, the dollar amount of the missing assets can, and should be, charged to that department's monthly expenses. Any such charge will stand out because it will not have been budgeted. It is highly likely that within days of the charge being shown, the department head will have done enough work to notify the accounting department of what really happened so a correcting entry can be made and the charge reversed. Assigning specific responsibility is the only way to induce managers to communicate on a regular basis with the accounting department regarding asset acquisitions, transfers, and dispositions.

 ## ZOMBIE ASSETS

In theory, it is impossible for significant pieces of PP&E to be physically present without a corresponding record on the books of account. After all, vendors do not usually provide gifts of hard assets to their customers.

However, in practice, when one takes a complete physical inventory of PP&E, there will be items that simply are there—but such items can**not** be located on the existing property register. To coin a phrase: "Property Happens."

In one sense it makes no difference how something came to be in the company's control without an appropriate accounting entry having been made. Internal controls should stop the loss of assets, and few people give much thought to the "spontaneous" appearance of "new" assets. But the existence of zombie assets, while maybe not as serious as the loss of assets that are now ghosts, is itself a symptom of poor controls.

Let us look at just a couple of ways this can happen.

First, many companies have stringent limits on the acquisition of capital items, often requiring relatively high-level approval for even relatively small items. A plant manager who can hire a $65,000 quality engineer is not permitted to spend more than $15,000 on testing equipment that will improve quality. Cash is cash and it never ceases to amaze this author how some firms treat capital dollars as somehow being different from expense dollars. Nonetheless, "the rules are the rules" and if the plant manager *has* to have a piece of equipment and cannot wait (in some instances for three months or more) for corporate approval, the answer is easy. Ask the vendor to split the invoice into two pieces, say of $8,000 payable one month and $7,000 payable the following month. The equipment is ordered, arrives, put on the floor, and the total cost charged to expense of the quarter. Maybe this was not what was anticipated when the rules were put into effect, but, as mentioned above: property happens.

A second example would be where a vendor promises to accept a trade-in and reduces the price of the new asset to recognize the trade-in. But in this case the vendor really does not want the asset, just the new order at a small discount representing the value of the trade-in. The vendor invoice shows the trade-in allowance and this time the accounting department is on the ball and retires the old asset from the books, with a corresponding gain or loss. Since the vendor did not want the trade-in, and leaves it with the customer, we now have a zombie asset, physically there but not on the books.

A third example shows still another cause. In a large machine shop environment we have seen that many fully depreciated assets will still be in use. If a critical piece of equipment breaks down, it is very common to use a part from another old, but similar asset, to repair it. This has been known to happen in transportation where a fleet of buses, trains, or planes is kept running by having parts from older units used as a source of spare parts.

Sometimes, a very creative plant engineer will see how to upgrade and improve a piece of equipment, perhaps by combining two old units into one new higher-volume piece of equipment, effectively custom designing and building the asset for the special purpose. If the rebuilding takes place within the factory, with existing maintenance staff, it is easy to see that a "new" unit will now be on the factory floor, turning out production every day. The physical makeup of this unit will in fact be parts from two or more fully depreciated assets, items that may in practice have been retired on the books but physically retained "just in case." Two years later an inventory of PP&E is taken, the new asset found and tagged, but there simply is no record in the financial records of how the piece of equipment got there.

Finally, in dealing with office furniture and fixtures, which virtually every company has, whether in manufacturing, service, or distribution, individual assets may have been acquired in bulk (e.g., ten desk chairs). Each chair may be worth only $200, but the company has a $1,500 capitalization cut-off. Some accountants capitalize the whole order because it is over $1,500. Other accountants look at the individual chair and say it is not worthwhile trying to control a single $200 chair over a period of years; therefore they charge the total invoice to expense. Now we have ten chairs, scattered throughout the office with no record on the property register. But when a physical inventory is taken often these individual chairs will be picked up as an asset on hand, even though originally it had been charged to expense.

 ## NETTING OUT GHOST AND ZOMBIE ASSETS—IS IT PERMISSIBLE?

We have assets on the books we cannot find, and assets we find that are not on the books, at least in identifiable form. We have taken an inventory from the existing asset listing, checked off the items we have found, and marked at least preliminarily the ghost assets. We have identified, with a description, the zombie assets we found that do not appear, at least directly, on the asset register.

At this point we really have three lists:

1. Assets on the books that we have found
2. Assets on the books that we have not found (ghost assets)
3. Assets that we have found that are not on the books (zombie assets)

The first thing to do is price out the list of ghost assets, and the corresponding annual depreciation charges. Since we do not know when the items went missing, we do not know how many years of depreciation have been overstated, or in which accounting period the amounts should have been written off.

Resolving this will become one of the accounting issues to be solved as part of the reconciliation process.

The second step is to obtain an estimate of the current fair value of the zombie assets, which were found. This estimate probably cannot be performed by the accounting staff. Two options offer themselves. One can ask the purchasing and engineering staff to provide their best estimate. Alternatively one can engage a valuation specialist, one who deals in machinery and equipment, and ask again for a best estimate. You do not need, at this point, to have a definitive answer on the specific value of each zombie asset. What you are striving for is to see how much difference, if any, there is between the dollar amounts on the two lists. In the best-case scenario the dollar value of the ghost assets approximates the dollar value of the zombie assets.

The second and more likely situation is that the dollar value of the ghost assets exceeds the estimated fair value of the zombie assets, in which case a write off or impairment charge will be necessary.

In the very unlikely situation that the zombie assets' value exceeds the missing ghost assets, it is unlikely that the company will be able to write up the dollar amount of PP&E. The only question then is how best to correct the property register, which we discuss ahead.

Netting Out Overages and Shortages

[Author's note: Please note that the views to be expressed here are those of the author, and may not be fully subscribed to by generally accepted accounting principles (GAAP) purists acting as auditors. It seems to this author that if we really want to have principles rather than rules, the principle of control over PP&E should be the guide, not arbitrary rules made up for other purposes. Keep in mind that all of accounting is an artificial construct, not an immutable physical law of the universe like $E = MC^2$.]

We now come to an accounting conundrum that must be resolved.

The easy and straightforward way would be to charge off to expense the net book value of all the ghost assets, set up the zombie assets on the property register with zero net book value, and move forward. This is conservative and undoubtedly would receive approval from many rules-oriented auditors. Zero judgment needs be applied and the entries can be verified and validated by the most junior auditor on the staff.

There is but a single problem with this approach. There are few CFOs and Corporate Controllers who willingly will go down this path. The reason is simple. If the missing ghost assets are perhaps 15% of all PP&E (which is what we find in many companies when a complete PP&E inventory is taken) the charge to expense will be both large, and unanticipated by directors, management, and shareholders. For practical purposes any financial manager who made the necessary entries described previously would effectively be signing his own resignation letter.

Admitting that past lack of control of PP&E had led to a current substantial writedown is an admission that there was poor internal control in the past. The fact that SOX statements have been signed saying that internal control has been present, and that the audit firm agreed, is perhaps setting the stage for the company, and the individuals involved, seeing a class action suit by hungry legal sharks being filed against them. In other words, the very writedown of missing assets is *ipso facto* an admission of past mistakes. Corporate mistakes in today's environment are all too often followed by class action lawsuits, with the lawyers looking for a massive dollar settlement to go away.

We see two different possible solutions, the first radical but it solves the problem, while the second in effect "kicks the can down the road." My preferred solution is to net out the write-offs from ghost assets with the pick-ups from zombie assets.

NETTING OUT GAINS AND LOSSES

My argument is that in the past the bookkeeping or accounting for PP&E might have been a little sloppy, but realistically most items of PP&E neither disappear nor arise spontaneously. Consequently, the existence of ghost and zombie assets is evidence of poor accounting, but not of true poor internal control. In other words, the company's assets have in fact been both physically *protected*, and undoubtedly *maintained* sufficiently to function as they were expected to by the system of internal control.

The Committee of Sponsoring Organizations of the Treadway Commission (COSO) developed the following definition of internal control:

> "A process, effected by an entity's board of directors, management, and other personnel, designed to provide reasonable assurance regarding the achievement of objectives in the following categories:
>
> ■ Effectiveness and efficiency of operations
> ■ Compliance with applicable laws and regulations
> ■ Reliability of financial reporting"

By definition, if there are both ghost and zombie assets then the accounting records are in error. But does this signal a true failure of internal control? Probably not.

Look at the three bullet points which represent the objectives of an internal control system. The errors in the property ledger can hardly have affected the "effectiveness and efficiency of operations." Production in the shop, and operations in the office, are in no way compromised if the milling machine was improperly accounted for, or if the desk should have been capitalized but was charged off to expense.

Similarly, it would be a stretch to say that "applicable laws and regulations" were violated simply because assets were possibly misclassified in the property ledger. Certainly over the past 30 years that the Foreign Corrupt Practices Act (FCPA) has been in effect, requiring accounting controls, nobody has been sued by the government for unintended errors in the property ledger. Perhaps a WorldCom situation, where the company deliberately falsified the assets to increase reported earnings, would be a violation of the FCPA. However, it would be hard to convict anyone under the FCPA guidelines simply for sloppy accounting records on PP&E.

It is the last bullet point, the "reliability of financial reporting," where poor property records fall within the ambit of internal control. Auditors year after year tell clients "You really should take a physical inventory of PP&E and reconcile it to the books." Yet this recommendation hardly ever gets done. This suggests that audit firms themselves do not view poor PP&E records as being sufficiently important to withhold certification.

In other words if the auditors really thought that the underlying reliability of overall financial reporting was at risk—because of a poor property ledger—they would not sign off on the financial statements year after year. So at this point we are really involved in a discussion about materiality, as much as the letter of the law concerning regulations and applicable statutes. Nobody can argue that you want poor property records; all you can say is that investors and creditors are not being materially misled.

It is for these reasons that we feel it is appropriate to net out the gains and losses, offsetting the ghost assets with the fair value of the zombie assets. It may not be strictly according to GAAP, COSO, and FCPA, but all the previous errors were never considered serious enough to preclude acceptance of the earlier financial statements. Why now suddenly insist on a much higher standard? Put a different way, management and auditors turned a blind eye to poor record keeping on PP&E. Now that we want to fix it, why insist on a higher standard that, in itself, will discourage management from undertaking the required steps?

As noted, if companies are forced to charge to expense the net book value of ghost assets, and cannot write up the fair value of zombie assets, it is highly doubtful that a once and for all clean-up will ever take place. This leads to the third option mentioned before.

PERFORMING THE INVENTORY AND RECONCILIATION PIECEMEAL

In the long run there will be some additional costs incurred if the inventory and reconciliation is performed for less than the company as a whole. The problem is stated easily, although not solvable quite as readily. As noted before, assets are often transferred within a company and the accounting department not notified. Consequently, the property ledger shows an asset as being in Department 10 of Building 3, whereas in reality it is in Department 50 in Building 2.

If you take the inventory by building, or by department, the asset will show up as a ghost asset in Department 10, and as a zombie asset in Department 50; of course the two net out. All that is really required is to make an entry on the property ledger showing the current location, and no debit or credit entries are required.

If, however, you take the initial inventory in Building 3, and postpone taking the inventory in Building 2 until the following year, you will be showing a ghost asset on the books for Building 3. This despite the fact that the asset has not gone missing, it is just not where the ledger says it should be. The final reconciliation, therefore, really could not be performed until the total company was inventoried and all reconciling items found.

Keep in mind that finding an asset missing in Building 3, and then locating it in Building 2, is a situation that can be corrected internally, with absolutely no impact on the books and records with respect to external financial reporting. As discussed earlier, it really is important to have the proper location for all assets to facilitate the responsibility for asset control. But an error in location does not affect depreciation expense in total for the company; admittedly internal cost accounting for pricing and inventory valuation may be off but from the perspective solely of external reporting location errors can be ignored.

By taking the inventory in stages, there is one great advantage that should be recognized, although probably not discussed too loudly. That is, as discussed previously, there is no real way of reconciling what appear to be possible ghost and zombie assets until the entire firm has been inventoried. So, if you are going to spread this over a five-year period, during that time frame it will be hard to develop a final company-wide reconciliation. The answer will probably be to make no entries for present and missing assets.

This postpones any day of reckoning and buys time for discussions with the audit committee and external auditors. "We're working on it" is certainly better than "We will try to get to that next year," particularly when next year never seems to come around. But in terms of actual internal control, a half-completed reconciliation realistically is nothing but a work-in-progress. If there is not immediate pressure from the board of directors or the audit firm this practical solution will appear very attractive.

The two downsides are that until finished you really cannot say you have effective internal control over PP&E. In addition even more importantly, if the entire process of taking the physical inventory requires five years, the final reconciliation across the entire company will be somewhat harder. This is due to the fact that within that five-year time frame, there will have been numerous transactions, additions, deletions, and transfers. These will only make the final adjustments harder, trying to keep track of the intervening actions that occurred between the start and finish.

My recommendation is to try and accomplish the company-wide inventory within a one-year time frame, even if the actual reconciliation and booking of any adjustments is carried over to a second year. For those with limited resources, who want to show they are "doing something" without risking a major accounting entry to write off missing assets, the five-year program will have a certain appeal.

 ## SUMMARY

Reconciling a physical inventory to the existing property records is a major task, simply to perform. Then, the results are very likely to be negative in terms of measuring and reporting on past performance.

In an ideal environment, say a private company with no outside share-holders or creditors, the best way of performing the reconciliation is to write off the ghost assets, write up the zombie assets, and take a charge for the net difference.

This may not be in compliance with GAAP. Given enough time it is possible to relate zombie assets in some way to existing entries on the ledger, and offset one with the other. There is, however, no known solution for true ghost assets other than to take a charge to earnings.

At the same time as the inventory is taken and reconciled, it would be desirable to review the existing lives for assets not yet fully depreciated. It is highly likely that lives can be extended, reducing annual depreciation charges and partially offsetting any write-off of ghost assets.

CHAPTER NINE

Fixed Assets in a Business Combination

C URRENT ACCOUNTING RULES SPELL out in detail the requirements for a buyer to allocate the purchase price based on the fair value of each acquired asset. This is sometimes called a purchase price allocation (PPA). In this book we can only cover the aspects of a PPA that deal with Property, Plant, and Equipment (PP&E). Valuation of intangibles is covered in detail in the author's book *Executive's Guide to Fair Value.*[1]

The basic accounting rules for all PPAs are covered in Accounting Standards Codification (ASC) 805-20-30-1 which provides:

> The acquirer shall measure the identifiable assets acquired, the liabilities assumed, and any noncontrolling interest in the acquiree at their acquisition-date fair values.

As can be seen, the key words are "acquisition-date fair values." There is an absolute requirement, therefore, that the buyer of a target company determine the fair value of all PP&E owned by the target company as of the acquisition date. As will be discussed in this chapter, there are essentially two ways to meet this requirement.

1. The least expensive is simply to carry over the target's net book value as the starting fair value of the asset.
2. The most accurate approach is to have the PP&E valued by a valuation specialist. In turn, valuation specialists sometimes apply cost indexes to the original cost, and in other cases actually determine the fair value using established valuation techniques.

The choice as to which course to pursue has to be made by the acquirer, after a full and frank discussion with the independent accountant, the outside auditor. A discussion with a qualified machinery and equipment appraiser should also provide input into what has to be, in the final analysis, a cost/benefit analysis.

 ## CARRYOVER OF TARGET'S BOOK VALUE

As a professional appraiser many clients are surprised when I suggest that they forego a detailed appraisal and recommend that they simply carry over the net book value directly from the target company's books. For this to work, to comply with GAAP (generally accepted accounting principles), we have to show that the book value of the PP&E on the seller's books is close enough to fair value that any divergence would not be material.

Most readers will have had numerous discussions with their auditors about what is and is not material; we do not need to recapitulate those discussions and we simply assume that readers are willing to accept a reasonable approach to materiality. The basic rule that we recommend can be stated as follows:

> If the net book value of acquired PP&E is less than 10% ± of the total purchase price there is no need to perform a detailed valuation on the PP&E. The target's net book value is going to be "close enough" that there is no justification for incurring the out-of-pocket cost of a detailed appraisal.

Service type companies usually have little in the way of PP&E other than office furniture and fixtures (including computers), and sometimes leasehold improvements. The accounting lives used by the target probably were too short; however, the book value is relatively low relative to the value of the company and the transaction. The fact is that if we use the FASB's (Financial Accounting Standards Board's) definition of fair value, an "exit price" the value of used office equipment and furniture including computers is *very* low. In practice, many companies living within tight financial constraints often acquire used furniture and equipment because there is little obsolescence (other than for electronics) and real bargains are often available in the used market. Consequently, carrying over net book value of PP&E is unlikely to be off by more than one to two percent of the acquisition price.

Interestingly, when we have been hired to perform a detailed valuation of PP&E the new fair value often turns out to be quite close to book value for most assets. As discussed in Chapter 1, this outcome is probably the result of some offsetting items. Nonetheless, there often is relatively little write-up, or write-down, of PPE from the target's net book value after performing a detailed valuation.

Why does this phenomenon exist? As mentioned, accounting lives based on tax provisions are usually far short of the true economic life, other than for computers and related items. The Internal Revenue Service (IRS) permits relatively fast write-off of technology so even though the value of personal computers probably is overstated, the overstatement is not likely to be significant. For desks, file cabinets, and so forth, the truth is that they simply do not wear out. New designs may make a 25-year-old desk look "old" but functionally it will be just as good today as it was on day 1. To sum up, technology assets have too long a life and office furniture and fixtures have too short a life.

Production machinery and various types of equipment similarly tend to have useful lives far in excess of standard tax lives. Most manufacturers have to maintain their equipment simply to maintain tolerances or production quality. With good maintenance, machine tools and production equipment can retain their utility for decades. Process equipment often is upgraded at the same time routine maintenance is performed, in order to maximize throughput and reduce product costs.

A further complication in revaluing assets acquired in a business combination is that a lot of the items in the asset register probably could not be found, if a detailed reconciliation were undertaken. This subject of comparing the books to actual assets is covered in Chapter 8. There are likely to be a substantial number of items on the books that are missing—perhaps traded in and not recorded, or transferred to another location again with no record having been processed. Offsetting these ghost assets are what we refer to as zombie assets, which are physically present, but not on the books. These latter sometimes appear because they were charged to expense, and not capitalized. Sometimes assets are transferred in—comparable to the assets transferred out—and no entry had ever been made.

Taking all these factors into consideration, unless PP&E is truly a material portion of the total purchase price, we do not recommend a full valuation. There is, however, a half-way step that is often used, and at far lower cost, with approximately equivalent accuracy most of the time. This is the application by valuation specialists of cost indexes to the original cost of acquisition.

 ## APPLYING INDEXES TO THE TARGET COMPANY'S ASSET REGISTER

The decision to index costs should be made jointly among the auditor, the company, and the valuation specialist. While far less expensive than a detailed *de novo* appraisal, it nonetheless involves significant resources and should not be undertaken unless everyone is in agreement.

Assuming the decision is made to utilize indexing to approximate the fair value of the acquired PP&E the first thing that an appraiser will do is to ask for the existing asset register of the target company. She will make a spot check of certain high-dollar-value items to see approximately how accurate the listing might be. This spot check would involve going out and physically inspecting the assets, seeing not only that they are there but also estimating the current condition.

Assuming the register looks reasonably reliable, the appraiser then looks for two key pieces of information: (1) the original date of acquisition and (2) the original acquisition cost. This, of course, is in addition to the basic description of the asset, including serial number and other unique identifying characteristics.

If the requisite information is available, the appraiser then can appropriately determine the current fair value of the assets through the application of indexes. Whole books have been written about the development and use of various types of indexes, and the overall subject of indexing is outside the scope of this book.

Suffice it to say that a wide variety of cost indexes are available to the valuation specialist and part of her knowledge base is the ability to utilize the most appropriate index for each type of asset. It is apparent that cost trends in the electronics industry are far different from those in the petroleum industry, and the construction industry shares few characteristics with say the printing business.

Assuming that appropriate indexes are available for the type of assets being addressed, it is fairly simple to input the index, by year of acquisition, into a computer. One then multiplies the original cost of the asset by the appropriate index for the stated year of acquisition. The index would have relative costs for each year; the computer program would select the index for the year of acquisition and multiply the original cost by the index to arrive at an estimate of the cost today for the asset on hand.

The asset register would have the accumulated depreciation based on the original cost and, all else being equal, the computer would calculate a corresponding amount to arrive at a net current value for the asset.

This use of indexes dramatically reduces the cost of determining a current value for machinery and equipment, as well as office furniture and fixtures, in contrast to a full appraisal to be discussed ahead. The tradeoff, however, is certainly less accuracy, so the question then becomes "how accurate should the new asset register be?"

As is discussed in Chapter 3, most company asset registers are not particularly accurate, so updating the costs of an inaccurate listing only carries forward all existing errors. Following the medical dictum of "Do No Harm," indexing an existing asset record certainly does not make things worse. The risk is that the "new" values may appear to be more accurate than they really are.

 ## INACCURACIES IN THE TARGET'S ASSET PROPERTY REGISTER

We stated that there were two requirements that are necessary for indexing to be permitted. The asset register in addition to the description must have (1) the original cost and (2) the original date of acquisition. What happens in practice is that the cost and acquisition date often do *not* represent the original amount paid to the vendor. Instead we often find that the amounts shown in the cost field really are "allocated costs" based on a prior acquisition.

Many companies, or divisional units of companies, have changed hands one or more times. Prior managers, appropriately following then-current accounting rules had revalued the assets at the time of the prior acquisition and used the *transaction* date in the *acquisition* date. Consequently, what the asset register shows as date and cost of acquisition are really no more than an estimate of value, not cost, at the time of the prior transaction.

Unfortunately, cost indexes cannot appropriately be applied to estimates of value with a date that reflects only when a prior acquisition transaction occurred. The basic structure of cost indexes is derived from actual reported transactions between buyers and sellers. The Consumer Price Index is developed by having shoppers go to stores and record actual selling prices for a specific basket of goods or services. Then the relative costs can appropriately be related to similar assets (products and services) purchased in prior periods. The difference between the old costs and the new current costs is the basis of the index showing the price change.

But it should be clear that an allocated value, derived from an accounting convention, does not in any way reflect an actual buyer-seller transaction for the original asset, an amount that is the only sound basis for application of cost indexes. If the only information available on the target's property ledger represents an allocated purchase price from a previous transaction, the appraiser really should not apply a cost index, and other means of developing current fair value must be found.

There is one additional problem with cost indexes, one that is not usually given sufficient weight. Cost indexes cannot effectively reflect improvements in technology. Taking personal computers as an example we can compare the price today of an Apple MacBook Air with an Apple computer sold in 2002. The price, in absolute dollars, has probably been reduced over an eight- to ten-year period. A good computer cost index will have captured the price reduction in dollars. There is no index, however, which will measure accurately the *improvements* in speed, capacity, and capability that the new unit has in comparison to the old one.

A similar phenomenon is faced by the Department of Commerce in developing the Consumer Price Index, where automobiles represent a significant portion of total expenditures. Every year Detroit comes out with new models, often with a higher sticker price. But the companies assert that this year's new model is "better" than last year's and the "improvements" are used to justify the higher price tag—with the consequent argument by the manufacturer, "Well, we really did not raise prices at all, you are just paying for a better product, one with newer and improved features."

As an example, a navigation device that was extra last year is included in this year's base price, thus providing additional "value" to the buyer this year. This argument, of course, is made whether or not the individual customer of the new model wants, needs, or uses the now standard navigation system. The issue for the people constructing the price index is to determine how much of the list price increase pertains to the navigation device and how much is an actual straight price increase.

This is but one of the many problems facing statisticians who devote their careers to price index construction. Financial executives with a long memory can recall the Securities and Exchange Commission (SEC) and FASB experiments with price level accounting in the late 1970s, where the choice of an index could make the company look good, or instead, poorly run. Since then cost and price indexes have not been so much under public scrutiny, but the conceptual problems of developing indexes in periods of technological change have not gone away.

Appraisers who rely on cost indexes to develop current fair values for machinery and equipment are usually quite sensitive to these issues. They almost always will stand back, examine the preliminary value indications, and adjust them as necessary, based on their professional experience. In other words, indexing should not, and is not, a "black box," with indexes and costs going in and fair values coming out. Indexing is a moderate cost alternative to a full-scale valuation, and in many situations will be sufficient for a PPA.

 ## DETAILED VALUATION OF PROPERTY, PLANT, AND EQUIPMENT

While we cannot in this chapter describe every step that an appraiser has to take to develop a complete valuation of a target's PP&E, we can at least indicate the key steps, with an explanation as to why they are performed.

In effect, when an appraiser is starting from scratch, the first step is a listing of the assets actually on the factory, office, or IT floor. Identification of the assets, by manufacturer and serial number is made, as well as recording the physical location of the asset. This listing is fairly time consuming, and since appraisers charge on the basis of time, not on the value of the assets they value, smaller low-dollar items are usually omitted. This ties into the recommendation made throughout the book that companies adopt a relatively high minimum capitalization threshold.

This is the reason that if there is a good property register, with a reasonably high degree of accuracy, the appraiser would start with that, saving time in the task of listing. Forty years ago, before video cameras and computers, appraisers literally went out into the field with a clipboard to list the assets.

To show how valuation techniques have changed, the author was told 40 years ago by an "old-timer" who had started well before World War II, that "in his day" appraisers literally would count the number of bricks in a building, then develop the cost of the building by obtaining costs for bricklaying, and so forth. Today, of course, most appraisers will use a building cost guide that provides square foot construction costs for all types of structures, with geographical multipliers to allow for regional labor and material costs.

While it would be hard to find an appraiser today who regularly lists manually on a clipboard, videotaping is an often used short-cut. In fact, in terms of providing a "Proof of Loss" to an insurance company, a video tape is an excellent, and low-cost, way of demonstrating what you owned at the time of the taping. We personally recommend videotaping for home use, as well as for nonprofits and smaller businesses who may not wish to pay for a detailed appraisal. Be sure to keep the videotape apart from the assets being recorded.

Once the appraiser has written down the description of the asset—or obtained it from the existing asset register—she will also record her estimate of the *condition* of the asset. As an example, if you have a numerically controlled milling machine the appraiser will ask the appropriate plant engineer or maintenance superintendant to indicate the maintenance history, and the degree to which the unit has suffered both normal "wear and tear" as well as any unusual problems.

There are really two quite different, and separable, types of depreciation that an appraiser takes into account. The first and easiest to understand is the physical condition, which is obvious. A used piece of production equipment is worth less than a new item, and the value often will decline more or less proportionately with age. So a ten-year-old milling machine will be worth less than a two-year-old piece of similar equipment. Assuming a correlation between age and physical condition is reasonable, your own automobile is a good example. Even with 15,000 miles on each of a 2006 and a 2010 pickup truck, the older vehicle probably would sell for less on a used-car lot.

The second thing looked at in the physical inspection is the *functional* utility of the equipment. For assets with little technological change, using common machine tools as an example, a well-maintained 30-year-old lathe will probably perform the same functions with the same tolerances as a more modern lathe.

But take a semiconductor "fab" plant. The physical output today from a 15-year-old facility that was "state-of-the-art" when newly constructed will be the same silicon wafer, say of 60 mm. But today's fab plants produce 300-mm wafers. The unit cost of semiconductors produced from the larger wafer is substantially less expensive than the identical item produced from the smaller wafer. The technological improvements involved in making larger wafers flow through to the output and cost of the end product.

Determining the fair value of the older plant, therefore, by applying an index to the original recorded cost, or direct pricing the assets by current vendor quotes will give you a number, but it will not be fair value. All you will have is "the cost in today's dollars to rebuild the existing asset." Assume perfect maintenance, because of the need to maintain tolerances, and you have replicated the original asset in today's dollars.

But would anybody pay, today, that amount? If a third-world country wanted to dip their toe into the semiconductor market they probably would buy an existing "used" facility, at some sort of negotiated price. Absent a third-world market it is hard to see who would pay today's dollars for yesterday's asset capability and productivity.

The only way to get the true value of the existing smaller facility to reflect actual demand is to assess the reproduction cost with a penalty that reflects the difference in the unit cost of production. So, just with artificial numbers for the example, assume a single semiconductor made from a 300-mm wafer costs $1.00, while the cost per unit is $1.25 from the 60-mm facility. We would take the present value of the $0.25 cost differential for all projected volume from the old small facility and subtract it from the new reproduction cost.

Now, from the perspective of a company that was going to expand capacity in semiconductors, they should be indifferent between paying a low up-front cost for the older 60-mm facility or a higher price for the new 300-mm plant. The unit cost of the output from the two facilities should be the same. Obviously, other characteristics will affect the final acquisition decision of a prospective investor, but in terms of fair value the valuation specialist will have properly adjusted the older technology to reflect current economics.

The best way to look at this concept is to realize that when there have been major technological improvements, in terms of process, the value of an older facility will be adversely affected. By the same token, if one has a production facility that has undergone no, or even minimal, changes in technology, the fair value of the existing older facility is going to be pretty much a function of age and condition.

Once the valuation specialist has inspected the plant, and the assets, identifying the make, model, serial number, date of acquisition, and condition, as well as understanding any changes in technology, then the real effort begins. The next step, usually performed back at the appraiser's office, is to determine the current cost of the indentified equipment; some items have had significant price increases over the year, while others, IT assets, for example, have historically had price decreases. The value today is a function of today's price, less depreciation from all causes.

To repeat what is discussed elsewhere because it is so often misunderstood, for an appraiser, depreciation is *not* what accountants calculate. Depreciation for financial reporting is a more or less arbitrary allocation of original cost over some assumed time period.

Depreciation to an appraiser represents the actual diminution in utility of the asset from both physical use and functional obsolescence, if any. Thus, a ten-year-old piece of production equipment for which an accountant might have originally assigned a 15-year life, may still have ten additional years of useful life. This estimate of an additional ten years utility is premised on an assumption of good maintenance, an assumption that is based on observed maintenance practices at the facility. Some companies are religious about preventive maintenance, which stretches out useful lives, while others are prepared to replace production equipment more frequently, anticipating that the newer equipment would be more productive. The appraiser does not make value judgments, and in effect reports only what is.

With a description of the machine, the current cost of a similar item, and an estimate of the remaining useful life, it is easy to determine the current fair value of the asset. The appraiser determines from suppliers, or other sources, what the cost is today of the type of equipment actually on the floor. That is why the serial number and model number are important. If you call Cincinnati Milacron to find out what the cost would be today for a machine they had made ten years ago, they will need the model and serial number to identify the existing asset and determine which model in today's line is closest to that asset.

From the replacement cost provided by the manufacturer, the appraiser then determines the effective remaining life of the existing asset, based on age and condition. This is strictly a judgment call, dependent in the final analysis on the professional experience and skill of the appraisal specialist. The resulting dollar amount now represents the true fair value of the individual assets in the facility. There may well be additional value to reflect the fact that the assets are fully installed, debugged, and running. Again, the only way to obtain this is through the professional judgment of the appraiser.

From the perspective of one of the FASB's theoretical market participants to whom an item might be sold, such a prospective buyer should be indifferent between buying a new asset at current price or the subject asset at its newly determined fair value, which would be much lower than the cost of a new asset and certainly with a shorter remaining useful or economic life.

In an extremely condensed fashion, the aforementioned is the thought process and the activities that a valuation specialist goes through if the valuation starts with a clean sheet of paper, rather than taking advantage of existing information. The final results of the detailed valuation will be very accurate, will be totally supportable in terms of audit, as well as useful for analysis and support of property tax and insurance reviews.

The problem is that in today's environment a detailed valuation such as we describe is very labor intensive, that is, having the appraiser literally going through the facility and recording the information manually. Using tape recorders and video recorders can speed up the process to a certain degree, at the possible expense of slightly less time spent evaluating physical condition. But the major time constraint is the pricing of the asset listing, determining the cost today of the subject asset, or its current replacement, and adjusting where necessary for technological improvements.

Even if the appraiser were given a perfect descriptive listing, substantial time and effort is involved in the pricing function. This pricing function is hard to delegate. The Internet is used as a reference source in many situations (both to identify used equipment dealer quotations, and actual auction prices) but for pricing a diverse complement of assets the Internet may not reduce total time significantly.

In practice, complete inventories of assets, for allocation of purchase price in a business combination, are fairly rare. Unless the PP&E represents the major asset category acquired, most companies (and their auditors) are satisfied with approximations, and most audit firms do not push for 100% accuracy. In today's business environment far more resources are devoted to determining what *intangible* assets should be valued at, and supporting the values, and useful lives of those intangibles. A steel mill, or an oil refinery, is the type of business where a detailed *de novo* inventory would be justified. Most other types of business, where PP&E may represent no more than 15 to 25% of total acquisition cost, cannot justify the substantial cost of a detailed appraisal, no matter how imperfect is the target's property register.

The argument that is made, and it is hard to overcome, is that if the target company and *its* auditor had lived with inaccurate property information on the target's books, the buyer, for whom the target is now a small part of the buyer's total, can certainly continue to use the same (imperfect) information.

Readers should not misconstrue what was just stated. We are not supporting use of poor information. We are saying that serious thought has to be given to a cost/benefit analysis. There are enough estimates and uncertainties in most financial statements that providing 100% accuracy, on 25% of the total, may not be worth the time and cost. Coming from someone with over 40 years of experience in valuation, it is easy to see that this recommendation is not based on strict self-interest.

SUMMARY

In a business combination, sometimes referred to as an M&A (merger and acquisition) transaction, current GAAP requires that the fair value of the acquired assets be determined. There are two basic ways of accomplishing this, assuming a decision is made not simply to carry over the target's net book value.

The two methods used by appraisers are indexing of existing cost records, and a complete *de novo* valuation. Indexing can work if the original cost and original acquisition date are available. If they are not available it may be necessary then to undertake a full-scale appraisal.

 ## NOTE

1. Alfred M. King, *Executive's Guide to Fair Value Profiting from the New Valuation Rules* (New York, NY: John Wiley & Sons, 2008).

10

Insurance for Fixed Assets

I N THIS CHAPTER WE cover the valuation requirements of fixed assets for purposes of insurance. This material, complete in itself, should be supplemented through discussions with insurance professionals because there are a lot of factors involved in the placement of the correct amount of insurance.

A basic principle of internal control is protection of the firm's assets by those responsible. Inasmuch as accidents do happen, it is incumbent on management to have sufficient insurance to try to make the company "whole" in case of loss. This is accomplished by purchase of insurance, in which the insurance company, in exchange for a premium, promises to reimburse the company in case of loss.

In exchange for a certain small loss (premium) the company is protected against an uncertain large loss (fire, etc.). A review of overall insurance coverage is essential as part of internal control, but is outside the scope of this book. Insurance professionals, often with the major brokerage firms like Marsh and Aon, have the expertise both to place the insurance and work with the company in all aspects of protection to mitigate the possibility of loss.

A word about "self-insurance." Many large companies are diversified geographically, which means that no single catastrophe (fire, flood, earthquake) will affect more than one location. Assuming the worst, large companies may be able to absorb the costs associated with a single catastrophe. Often they will determine that the cost of paying an outside insurance company is greater than any realistic estimate of a potential large loss. Such companies choose, consciously, not to purchase insurance and are prepared to pay for losses out of existing company assets or borrowing capacity.

As noted, many commentators refer to this as "self-insurance." A moment's thought, however, will realize that is a misnomer. The company has *no* insurance, it is in fact *un*insured. Certainly, "self-insurance" *sounds* a lot better to an investor or creditor than does the term "no insurance"; nonetheless, anyone who says they are "self-insured" actually has no insurance. Despite the fact that this may sound bad or weak, having no insurance may make perfect economic sense.

Insurance professionals, without exception, will tell you not to insure things that you can easily pay for. You do not want the premiums to be higher than the expenses they are insured against, and when you have lots of small losses it does not pay to buy insurance in advance. A company with a fleet of cars should not insure them against the risk of a tire blowout on a replacement cost basis. An insurance company can hardly process premiums that will be used to pay occasional claims for new tires costing no more than $100.00 each.

So, "no insurance," or call it "self-insurance" if you prefer, is a rational policy under certain circumstances. But whether you have no insurance and will pay your own claims or pay an insurance company to reimburse you for claims, you still have to know the value of the assets at risk.

That is the subject of this chapter, how to determine insurable values.

 ## USING THE MASTER PROPERTY RECORD FOR INSURANCE

The same property record used for depreciation and property tax assessments can be and should be used also for recording insurable values.

The input forms for property record software systems provide multiple input columns. Some may wonder why anything other than the original cost, and accumulated depreciation, is necessary in the property record. Certainly when asset control was on 4 × 6-inch cards, there was no room for property tax or insurance information. Today's personal computer–based fixed-asset accounting systems do have that capability, and we strongly support such use.

The property record can, and should, be used for the *placement of insurance,* and in case of need, provide the proof of loss. The actual placement of insurance, determining the exact limits, what is covered and what is not covered, and the resultant premium requires an expert on insurance, not a valuation specialist. So we show you how to determine the value of the assets at risk, not what kind of policy to have or with whom you should have it.

INSURABLE VALUES ARE NOT FAIR VALUE OR FAIR MARKET VALUE

For many individuals, who are not knowledgeable about assets and asset values, the concept that the same asset can have different values at the same time is sometimes hard to comprehend. Just one simple example should suffice here. When you buy property damage insurance on a building you do not pay a premium to cover the value of the underlying land or the foundation of the building. The reason is simple: Land does get destroyed in a fire, and the basement or foundation will also most likely not be materially affected. Though the purchase price of a building several years ago, or its fair market value (FMV) today incorporates both the land value and the foundation. For insurance, these have to be *excluded*.

Consequently, the property record for the building will be separate from the land (no depreciation on the land) but it will include the foundation. For insurance one must subtract the value of the foundation, thus arriving at a different amount than the total cost of the building or even its FMV today. Thus, for the building we need two separate columns in the property record, one for original cost and one for insurable value. As noted in Chapter 11 on Property Taxes, a third value is most likely to be appropriate for payment of property taxes. Once this is understood the confusion goes away, but one is still left with the need to develop the appropriate insurable values, and as discussed in the next chapter, assessable values.

The fundamental principle of insurable values is that you need an amount, which if paid upon loss, will make you as nearly whole as possible. Take a private car as an example. If you have a 2010 low mileage top of the line Toyota Camry XLE sedan, 6 cylinders, and want to sell it, Kelly Blue Book indicates in a private transaction you could expect to receive (as of the date this is written) $22,500. However, if your car was destroyed and you had to go to a dealer to replace it you would expect, again according to Kelly Blue Book, to have to pay some $27,400. This $4,900 differential represents in effect the difference between the bid and asked price or the dealer's margin for expenses and profit.

When you want to sell something you take the bid price and when you want to buy, assuming you are not in the business, you have to pay the ask price. The same holds true in the jewelry business or any business for that matter. In fact, how can a business survive if it buys and sells at the same price? What will cover the overhead, pay the salary of the owner, and hopefully provide a profit?

Getting back to the automobile example, if you insured your car for $22,500 and it was totaled, you would have to pay $4,900 more, unless you were willing to settle for something other than what you lost. Maybe there will be another used 2010 XLE Camry with low mileage in mint condition that you could find. But how much time do you have for shopping? How sure are you of the quality of a used car you would buy from a private party?

In short, to come out whole you should have insurance of $27,400 on the car. But if you were drawing up a personal balance sheet properly, and put down your car as an asset, you should only show the $22,500 as the value of the car, since if you sold it that is all you could reasonably expect to receive. For financial reporting and internal financial analysis, current FMV is totally relevant. For insurance, FMV while not irrelevant is also not appropriate.

HOW APPRAISERS DETERMINE INSURABLE VALUES

In our discussion of value and valuation principles, we indicated there were three ways, and only three ways, to determine the value of any asset. One of those three ways is often referred to as the cost approach. What it states is that the fair value, based on the cost to replicate an asset, represents the highest amount that anyone would pay, because the alternative is to go out and buy the same or a similar asset. So, for a building, if you have a 100,000-square-foot warehouse, and current construction costs for that type of building were $45 per square foot, then the maximum value of the building on the market would be $4.5 million, not including the land.

An owner could not sell the building for more, say $4.8 million, because prospective buyers would say, "I can build a brand-new building for $4.5 million so why should I pay your asking price of $4.8 million for your existing facility?" This disregards conceptual problems as to the desirability of the specific location, or that the existing building is available for immediate occupancy, while it would take ten months to build a new structure. But, as a generalization, the cost to acquire something is its maximum value, the most that someone would pay for it.

We use the cost approach in valuing income-producing assets as a reality check on the prospective income, and to compare to asking prices for existing assets in the market place. Now as far as insurable values are concerned we have to determine the cost of the assets because in case of loss we will have to replace them (i.e., buy them or build them). Thus, *we want to know what it would cost today to acquire the assets* that will be subject to the insurance policy.

Some readers may say: "Wait a minute. We are insuring used assets. Would an insurance company actually reimburse us for a *new* asset?" The answer of course is insurance companies would be reluctant to do that if for no other reason than that of "moral hazard," the temptation of an owner to cause a loss deliberately in order to get new assets for old.

Basically, insurance is designed in case of loss to make the insured "whole," not to turn them into a "winner." So, how do we determine the insurable values of used equipment, or real estate for that matter?

The term that appraisers use, in determining insurable values is "cost of reproduction new less depreciation," which turns into the short acronym CRNLD. The basic concept is the value of an existing piece of equipment can be determined by obtaining today's cost of the same item (reproduction) and *subtracting* "depreciation." The term "depreciation" as used by valuation specialists is NOT the same as accounting depreciation. In fact there is virtually no relationship between a more or less arbitrary accounting charge applied against the original purchase price, and the actual current condition of the asset, here, a piece of equipment or a building.

Why does it require a valuation specialist to determine insurable values? Why can accountants or plant engineers not perform that task? Determining the actual diminution in value due to physical wear, functional obsolescence, and loss of economic value involves knowledge that most accountants do not have. Certainly, plant engineers understand these concepts, but do not usually apply them on a regular basis.

Machinery and equipment specialists, as well as real estate appraisers (two separate valuation specialties) do work with these concepts all the time, have the research sources available, and are able to leverage experience from one client engagement to another. The biggest competition that appraisal companies face is not from accountants, or plant engineers, but rather from companies that do not know they need the knowledge that appraisers bring to the determination of values. Our biggest competition is prospective clients that do not believe they need help in determining insurable values.

We mentioned three reasons that the value of current assets differs from the same asset(s) if new. They are:

1. Physical wear and tear
2. Technological change, or functional obsolescence
3. Economic obsolescence

Physical Wear and Tear

Physical wear and tear is what most accountants think of when the term depreciation is used in a functional, not an accounting context. A machine tool suffers loss of tolerances simply by virtue of age, and how much it has been used. Think of an automobile. A car with 100,000 miles on it differs from a brand new vehicle of identical specifications. Yes, tires can be replaced, wipers changed, new muffler put on, and so forth, but no matter how well cared for, nobody would pay the same for a car with 100,000 miles as one with only 1,000 miles on it.

Depreciation from physical wear and tear, given normal use and reasonable maintenance policies, can usually be estimated on a more or less straight-line basis. Obviously, this timeframe is not determined by tax or financial accounting conventions, but is based on actual expected operating life.

Technological Change or Functional Obsolescence

Technological change or functional obsolescence is totally different from physical wear and tear. An easily understood example would be a personal computer. For practical purposes there is very little diminution of value from physical conditions in a personal computer, no matter how much it has been used or how old it is. A ten-year-old computer will perform just as well today as when it was brand new, at least on the functions performed ten years go. Sooner or later some of the chips, and other electrical components, may fail; even then a replacement will restore the unit essentially to its original condition.

But today's computers differ markedly from those of ten years ago. If you had stored a brand new computer in 2001, and took it out of the closet in 2011 for the first time, it would work perfectly, with 2001's software. It probably would not work well, if at all, with software currently in use in 2011. The technology of the hardware, and the associated software, has changed, and prospective users are unlikely to be satisfied with a ten-year-old computer, even in absolutely pristine condition.

It is possible to adjust the replacement cost of a new asset for the impact of technological change. Appraisers look at the operating costs and output of the new equipment, compared to the current costs and output of operating the subject asset. Then, using a discounted cash flow analysis, the cost penalty of the old asset and the net present value of the differential in operating expense or volume is subtracted from the cost of the new asset. Applying a factor for the age of the subject asset it is possible to estimate the economics of the current asset from that which would be present if a new asset were to be acquired. Basically, this is how appraisers determine the insurable value of machinery and equipment, electronic equipment, and almost all other asset categories. The exception is if there are significant external factors, what appraisers call economic obsolescence.

Economic Obsolescence

Economic obsolescence is usually defined as caused by factors *outside* the company. An example would be the most technologically up-to-date facility to make hula-hoops. Even as a state of the art factory, the real value of the assets, as a combination to produce a specific product, would be worth far less than its cost today. The reason is clear: There is very little demand for hula-hoops, so no matter how big, and how technologically efficient, the facility will be running way below capacity. Total revenue would probably not cover out-of-pocket costs, much less provide a profit.

In a situation such as this the value of the assets is a function of the actual expected future profits, discounted back to today at a rate equal to investors' expectations. The author was involved in a real situation similar to this one, dealing with a large amusement park. The replacement cost of the assets, primarily rides, was substantial, but the total attendance, and hence revenue, was insufficient to provide a normal return on the current replacement costs of the total assets employed. We had to reduce the replacement cost of the asset to reflect the expected economic return. Therefore, as valuation specialists, we applied an overall discount to reflect the economics (low attendance) of the specific property.

Now, in terms of insurance, if assets are not producing an economic return, it is not reasonable to expect an insurance company to reimburse you for the replacement costs, since it is extremely unlikely that one would take the insurance company check and reinvest in assets that are not expected to produce an economic return. We have all heard of strange fires, suspiciously convenient, that hit an unprofitable business. Rumors that the fire had been set in order to collect insurance may or may not be true, but the suspicions nonetheless are based in an understanding of real-world economics.

 ## INDEXING

If a company's fixed-asset records are not in good shape, it could pay to retain an appraisal firm to determine the insurable value of the assets. The savings in insurance premiums, and help in making a subsequent claim if the assets have been overinsured, could easily pay for the valuation. By the same token, if the assets have been underinsured, premiums will go up, but management can be sure that in case of loss the company will not be too much out-of-pocket. Overinsurance and underinsurance are both incompatible with good internal control.

Once assets are properly valued for insurance purposes, and appropriate insurance premiums are being paid, the next issue is to make sure that inflation (or even deflation) does not cause the values to become out of date. It would not be cost effective for a company periodically to hire outside valuation consultants to update insurable values every couple of years by conducting a brand new appraisal.

It is far better to apply *cost indexes* to the information in the property record. Most valuation firms have access to a number of cost indexes for a variety of asset types and industries. Properly applied, cost indexes can bring insurable values up to date very inexpensively, and with a degree of accuracy that insurance companies will accept and that companies can afford.

All of the current software systems can handle indexing and if nothing else this is sufficient reason to acquire and install modern fixed-asset software. However, a word of caution is in order.

Cost indexes measure changes in the cost of the assets or asset categories in the specific index. An oil price index can measure changes in crude prices, while a gasoline index is only valid for that specific commodity. An index of construction costs can only be applied to the specific type of construction named, since residential construction and commercial construction do differ. Finally, you can have an index of chemical industry construction costs, more limited in scope than an overall commercial construction cost index but more accurate for that specific asset base.

The essential element of a cost index is that it measures changes in cost of an asset. In constructing indexes there are always issues regarding changes in the product base, and this is exemplified by government efforts to construct an index of automobile costs. The industry, trying to keep the apparent price increases as low as possible, argues that this year's "improved" model, while costing more in absolute dollars than the same model did last year, also provides features not available last year. So if a Chevrolet Cruze costs $14,000 in 2010 and $14,700 in 2011 the question is, did costs rise 5% (105% of $14,000 = $14,700) or did the addition of a formerly optional, now standard, navigation system (retail price $350) "improve" the car. How the statistician answers this question affects the index and the resultant discussion in the press.

Questions about the cost of living have political ramifications, so a lot of effort and energy is spent on consumer price indexes. Business indexes, which are not nearly as visible, do not get this type of scrutiny, even though the same conceptual issues arise.

At the end of the day, whoever is developing a cost index has to make his or her determination about how changes in the underlying product affect the cost index. But, by the same token, a company consistently applying the same cost index each year, where there is not obvious bias one way or the other, will probably arrive at reasonable answers.

There is one aspect about indexing that must be both emphasized and understood. Indexes can only be applied to the original cost of the asset, based on the actual original year of purchase from the manufacturer. An example, if you have a Cincinnati Milacron milling machine purchased in 2000 for $100,000, then a machine tool cost index should give you an approximately correct insurable value in 2011. Keep in mind that cost indexes are updated each year, and if the base year for the index was 1990, then the insurable value in 2011 would be the 2011 index multiplied by the original cost and divided by the 2000 index.

Now look at what happens if instead of the original cost for the new item in 2000 we have an allocated amount arising from say a 2005 business combination. Some companies, when they buy another, put the "year of acquisition" as the merger date, and the "cost" as the amount determined in the 2005 appraisal required for the merger transaction.

What should not be done in 2011 is apply the cost index to the 2005 data and then assume that is the appropriate 2011 cost. The 2005 "cost" is actually for a used asset, not a new asset. So if a new milling machine in 2005 would have cost $110,000, the used asset might have gone on the books in 2005 for perhaps $65,000 depending on its condition at the time.

Applying a cost index developed from price trends for new equipment to a used piece of equipment will not provide a truly supportable value. Ideally, in this situation you would find an index of used equipment, which could properly be applied to the 2005 $65,000 used value. However, there are not all that many indexes of used equipment, because of the vast differences in condition. If someone told you that they wanted to sell you a 2009 Ford F150 truck, and provided no further information, it would be impossible to make an informed decision. You would want to know mileage, condition, and optional equipment including engine size and transmission. Given these variables, would it make sense to have an index of used trucks, much less used Ford F150s?

The solution to the problem posed here, regarding indexes and used equipment prices, is actually very simple. The acquiring company in a business combination should *retain* the seller's original cost and date of acquisition in the property file. Current software systems provide the necessary capabilities for entering this information. It is true that data will only be used for developing insurable values, and perhaps support for property tax assessments. But the cost of entering the data is minimal, and it costs nothing to maintain it into the future. When you want to use the property record for determining insurable values there is no substitute for the original acquisition date when the equipment was new, and the then purchase price.

PROOF OF LOSS

The appraisal business started in the 1890s when an insurance agent realized that companies were having trouble telling the insurance company, after a loss, just what was lost and how much it had been worth. In a stroke of genius they realized that a neutral third party could list every asset, with a full description, and then value it before any loss had occurred. This listing would not be kept at the insured's property, but in a warehouse maintained by the appraiser.

Then if and when there was a fire, or other loss, there would be no disagreement between the insurance company and the insured about either what was lost or what its value was. Thus, in one effort, the insured would know how much insurance to carry and would be neither overinsured nor underinsured. In case of loss, again there would be no dispute that certain assets had been lost; similarly the insured would not forget to file a claim for all assets whether they remembered them or not.

Human memory plays strange tricks. You, the reader, would be hard pressed this minute to describe *all* the assets in your living room at home or family room. In case of a total loss how would you be certain of being reimbursed for actual losses? You do not need to have a detailed listing prepared by a qualified appraiser.

What we recommend, and with today's technology it is simple to do, is that you buy an inexpensive video camera. Go around the house filming each room from all angles. With the audio you can describe any unusual or valuable items, even assigning an approximate value on the original tape. The one critical aspect is to put the final tape in a safe deposit box or any other secure storage away from the property! You do not want to lose the record itself as part of any future destruction.

Sometimes an appraiser will make a video record of the property being valued, if the current property record is not complete. With today's billing rates companies cannot afford to have appraisers make a detailed asset listing simply for a potential proof of loss. Forty years ago, when compensation was much lower, the vast majority of the work of a major appraisal firm was doing just that, detailed asset listings. Of course there were no computerized asset listings and the handwritten list was in many cases all that was available.

Today, the computerized property record should be in sufficient detail that it will be accepted by an insurance carrier both for determination of insurable values, and for any required future proof of loss.

 ## SUMMARY

Now, 40 years later, technology has eliminated the need for much of that detailed manual work in valuation. Technology has *not*, however, eliminated the same two basic needs that were apparent in 1890. Companies have to know how much insurance to carry. In addition, in case of loss they have to file a claim for actual assets lost.

Today's property record systems can easily provide this information if the correct original data is entered and maintained. Internal control systems should provide for periodic reviews of insurable values, and for making sure that a copy of the basic record is maintained off-site.

Developing insurable values can most economically be done by applying cost indexes to the original acquisition cost, based on the date of original purchase. Allocated costs developed as part of a purchase price allocation in a business combination will comply with generally accepted accounting principles (GAAP), but will not be sufficient for insurance purposes.

CHAPTER ELEVEN

Property Taxes—Personal Property and Real Estate

WARNING: THE LAWS AND court cases governing assessment of property vary widely by state. In most cases intangible assets are *not* taxed but in some states property tax assessments do include intangible values. Even worse, there may be different tax *rates* depending on whether the assessment is at the state, or at the local, level. Local counsel may be needed to resolve specific issues in a particular jurisdiction. A national professional service firm, such as Duff and Phelps or a Big Four accounting firm, has expertise that can be focused on specific tax issues. Here we can cover only general principles.

While there are a number of very good reasons for a company to have a good property record system, only a few can make an actual difference in terms of cash flow. These essentially are:

- Property taxes
- Insurance
- Component depreciation
- Maintenance

In this chapter we cover property taxes. Within this broad topic two key areas will be covered.

First is making sure that the information supplied to the local taxing authority does not overstate the true value of the asset(s). Simply copying over, on the appropriate tax form each year, the dollar amount of all items capitalized in that jurisdiction may overstate the "cost."

Second, it may be necessary to appeal the fair market values (FMV) determined by the taxing authority on which that year's taxes will be assessed. The only way to appeal will be from the company's own records, not those prepared and maintained by the taxing authority.

In virtually all jurisdictions property taxes are assessed at the local city or county level, with some states having what is called "unitary" assessment at the state level. Unitary assessments generally are applied to companies whose operations are spread out over an entire state, such as railroads, pipelines, and cable franchises. It would make little sense for 30 counties in a state each to try and determine the FMV of a few miles of railroad, 10 miles of pipeline, or 20,000 cable TV subscribers. In such instances it is much more efficient for the taxpayer to deal with one taxing authority; in such instances then the state allocates out the values to each jurisdiction on the basis of relative assets in that locality.

 ## REPORTING FAIR MARKET VALUES UPON ACQUISITION

Virtually every taxing jurisdiction relies on self-reporting of property additions and deletions. Annual reports are submitted, often as of January 1st, showing all new acquisitions, and any retirements, for the prior calendar year. Municipalities then keep records by taxpayer showing on a cumulative basis, by year of acquisition, what they consider to be the current value of the taxpayer's overall assets.

To arrive at an assessment value, *which is supposed to be at FMV*, most jurisdictions apply cost indexes to prior year acquisitions, in an effort to show what the "current cost" is of the assets still on hand. Implicit is the assumption that the current cost, based on indexed original cost is the FMV of the assets. Inasmuch as retirements have to be reported by year of original acquisition, the municipalities' records purport to show the total current value of all Property, Plant, and Equipment (PP&E) assets owned by the taxpayer as of the reporting date.

A moment's reflection reveals that the accuracy of the tax assessors' values is going to be a function of the accuracy of the cost indexes and the accuracy of the asset detail submitted by the taxpayer. Errors in either, or both for that matter, will cause companies to pay more tax than they need to.

Cost Indexes represent a shortcut to estimate current FMV as discussed in Chapter 10. The basic assumption of a cost index is that it purports to reflect changes in selling prices by vendors, purchase prices that would be paid today, were a company to acquire all prior assets at today's costs.

The construction of a cost index is both simple and complex, as shown by the federal government's attempts to develop the consumer price index that impacts such things as Social Security payments. It is simple because it takes a standard complement of assets each year and obtains current price quotes for each item in the index. Weights are usually assigned to individual components based on relative purchases, or use, of the specific item.

Thus, for example, assume a simple fruit and vegetable price index. Every year at the same time (to avoid seasonal influences) the person constructing the index would obtain prices from the local supermarket of carrots, potatoes, and lettuce. The relative weighting of carrots in the index would reflect the relative purchases of carrots by consumers in relation to all other fruits and vegetables a typical family buys.

So the first year of the index construction the statistician would determine typical purchase patterns (or sale patterns if this was to be a store index not a consumer index) of vegetables. If this were a national index then samples would have to be obtained from areas throughout the country since prices of oranges in Florida might differ from oranges in Alaska.

Whatever the final complement of the index, the maintenance of the index on a yearly basis would require getting new price quotes each year, assuming that relative consumption would not change. In other words, even if the price of oranges went up, and the price of lettuce went down, the index assumes constant relative consumption and that people would not substitute grapefruit for oranges or tomatoes for lettuce.

To the extent that relative purchases are not directly influenced by price changes such an index can faithfully reflect price changes in fruits and vegetables consumed by the average family. In the real world, however, prices do change behavior and this makes construction of price indexes quite difficult. In fact, statisticians devote entire lifetimes to refining indexes.

Readers at this point may ask themselves if the price of lettuce went up (because of a drought in California) but tomatoes produced locally had gone down, would we not use more of one and less of another? The answer, of course, is that prices do drive consumer behavior. But if the statistician re-balanced the index every year, it would be hard to have a price index; rather you would have an index of how much consumers spend on fruits and vegetables—which is not the same thing as a price index.

Now, to carry the analysis one step further, it is easy to assume that fruits and vegetables hardly change in content or format. A bunch of carrots from ten years ago is going to look identical to a bunch of carrots bought yesterday. A change in price from carrots ten years ago to today undoubtedly reflects only a change in price.

But now, keeping consumer expenditures in mind, what if we are trying to develop a price index of television sets. OOOOPS, we have a little problem. Ten years ago very few flat-screen televisions were sold, and the few flat-screen sets available were very expensive. Over the ten-year period, the price of television sets has gone down, the screen size has gone up, and Cathode Ray television sets will soon reside only in the Smithsonian. Everyone will have either a plasma or LCD set, with size depending on one's budget.

How do you develop a price index when the item itself is changing because of technology and customer demand? To put it in a nutshell, developing price indexes of technology items requires a great deal of professional judgment. The federal government has this problem in evaluating the consumer price of new cars. How much of a price increase is attributable to a new GPS system now made standard? Ten years ago no cars had GPS, now perhaps 50% have them. Undoubtedly, some of the total price increase in autos over that time period reflects new features, and the remainder of the price index reflects true price increases on a "like for like" basis.

In this book we are not trying to make you, the reader, into a statistician, only to point out in easily understood terms the real difficulties in developing, and then using price indexes. With respect to property taxes, municipalities do apply readily available indexes to all the types of assets owned by taxpayers. But can a price index capture price changes in machine tools where computer controls increase the price but also increase the productivity? The answer is that price indexes do a good job where changes in technology are absent, or even quite limited; indexes do a poor job where technology and productivity changes are great.

This digression was to put the problem of indexes into place, because of the tremendous reliance that municipalities place on the use of indexed original cost. Indexed costs can approximate FMV in certain cases, but in others are more than likely to *over*state assessed value relative to true FMV.

Municipalities do make one further adjustment. They apply a depreciation factor to the indexed historical cost to allow for the diminution in utility as an asset gets older and suffers physical wear and tear. Again, as in our discussion earlier about companies using tax depreciation lives for financial reporting, "rules of thumb" or arbitrary lives used by tax authorities simply do not (and cannot) measure actual reductions in value due to physical wear and tear and functional obsolescence.

The end result of these adjustments made by property tax authorities is their own estimate of FMV, not what the company itself might consider its true value.

Readers should keep in mind that in virtually all taxing jurisdiction property taxes are supposed to be collected based on an *ad valorem*[1] approach. As both statutes state, and court decisions have held:

> Fair Market Value is defined as the price for which property would exchange between a willing buyer and a willing seller, each having reasonable knowledge of all relevant facts, neither under compulsion to buy or sell, and with equity to both.

The question then has to be asked, "If you start with the original cost of an asset (purchased years ago), and have adjusted it upward by a cost index and downward by a depreciation factor, how close is the resulting amount likely to be to today's FMV?" It might only be a coincidence if the two amounts were close.

EQUITY AMONG TAXPAYERS

There is another factor that has to be considered. In many communities there is one major employer, and the property of that company represents a significant percentage of total taxable values. We have had clients in this exact situation; when the property of a major employer appears to be overvalued, particularly considering economic and functional obsolescence, there is a difficult problem. If one company is paying 40% or more of *total* tax receipts in a community, it may not help to get the assessment reduced. The total tax collections by the jurisdiction have to be maintained (schools, roads, police, etc.) and what happens is that the tax *rate* will have to be increased for everyone else. Further, the "other" taxpayers, who are the company's employees, will have their taxes go up immediately and directly.

Some companies, in this situation, decide not to appeal. A successful appeal will only reduce actual tax payments for the company, at the expense of employees feeling immediate pain. Overvalued industrial and commercial property often suffers economic problems, with concomitant layoffs. So the company is between the proverbial rock and a hard place. Shrugging off the tax burden directly onto the employees, at a time of layoffs, may not appear to be good community relations, even if it were to make technical financial sense.

This situation, while not uncommon, is only true when one employer in a community is the single largest taxpayer. In situations where there are a number of commercial and industrial properties, a reduction in the assessment of one probably will not be felt directly by other taxpayers.

Assessments are designed to spread the tax burden fairly among taxpayers. It is the actual amount of tax collections sought by the government that ultimately impacts taxpayers. Further, the absolute level of assessments is unimportant; it is only the *relative* assessments that count. It makes no difference in outlays or cash flow if tax assessments are at 50% of true FMV and the tax rate is $1.20 per $100 or if assessments are at 100% of FMV and the tax rate is $0.60 per $100.

So it is possible to live with assessments at any percent of FMV, as long as *everyone* is at the same percentage. The problem with assessments at less than 100% of FMV is that it is more difficult to compare properties. If your warehouse is assessed at 25% of value, while your neighbor is actually assessed at 20% of his value, you will be paying more than your fair share of taxes. All other things being equal the higher the relationship of assessed values to true FMV the better off are taxpayers in terms of equity. In the example cited here, determining the estimated FMV of an asset from an assessment may be difficult because the difference between a 20% and a 25% adjustment may not be clear—particularly since "values" are approximate and never exact.

 ## APPEALING PERSONAL PROPERTY TAX ASSESSMENTS

Speak to a knowledgeable assessor and you will find that a surprising number of assessments end up in court. It is hard to estimate what percentage of cases are won by plaintiffs (the taxpayer) and what percentage are won by the assessor (where the value stands). If you think you are overassessed and hence overtaxed going to court may be your best solution.

There is no reason to back down from a legitimate dispute with the taxing authorities. The reason is straightforward. Assessors, as government employees, are supposed to be neutral and unbiased. But in the final analysis their pay, and that of all their fellow government employees, is a function of tax collections. The more tax collected the more secure is the assessor in her job. Virtually all assessors do a good job, and are essentially neutral in their outlook. It is likely that in case of doubt many assessors may lean to a higher rather than lower assessment. It is these that can and should be challenged.

In some jurisdictions the assessment function is performed by an elected official, in others, assessors are only employees. In Virginia, the author's home state, the tax assessment function is held by an elected "Commissioner of the Revenue," a title that probably goes back to before the American Revolution. While elected assessors probably do not run, or get elected, on a platform of "I will collect more taxes," nonetheless government ultimately depends on tax revenues; tax revenues are a joint function of assessments and tax rates. Consequently, there can be a bias in favor of collecting more, not less, taxes, and this bias sometimes shows up in higher assessments.

As just discussed the purpose of assessments is to provide equity among all taxpayers, so too high an assessment means you are paying more than your fair share. Appealing an unfair assessment, and winning, simply puts you back where you were before the error.

INDEXED COSTS MAY NOT REFLECT FAIR MARKET VALUE OF PROPERTY, PLANT, AND EQUIPMENT

As discussed in Chapter 10 on insurable values of PP&E, the most cost-efficient way to *approximate* the current value of the assets is to apply appropriate cost indexes. There are many sources of indexes and some judgment must be used in choosing which to use. But once an appropriate index has been chosen, updating the estimate of current cost (assumed to be a proxy for FMV) is simply a matter of loading the index(es) on to the computer and pressing the right button.

Right or wrong, this essentially is what most assessors do to update their estimates of FMV, which is used as the basis for the annual assessment. As a result of the frailties of indexing, it behooves controllers or tax directors to review carefully the assessed values of major properties. Determine the company's own internal estimate of what you think the assets or plant might be worth and compare the two values. Perhaps the best way to decide where one can spend limited resources in reviewing tax assessments itself comes directly from generally accepted accounting principles (GAAP).

In reviewing assets for possible impairment, the Financial Accounting Standards Board (FASB) has laid out a number of what they call "impairment indicators" as follows:

> *360-10-35-21* A long-lived asset (asset group) shall be tested for recoverability whenever events or changes in circumstances indicate that its carrying amount may not be recoverable. The following are examples of such events or changes in circumstances:
>
> a. A significant decrease in the market price of a long-lived asset (asset group)
> b. A significant adverse change in the extent or manner in which a long-lived asset (asset group) is being used or in its physical condition
> c. A significant adverse change in legal factors or in the business climate that could affect the value of a long-lived asset (asset group), including an adverse action or assessment by a regulator
> d. An accumulation of costs significantly in excess of the amount originally expected for the acquisition or construction of a long-lived asset (asset group)
> e. **A current-period operating or cash flow loss combined with a history of operating or cash flow losses or a projection or forecast that demonstrates continuing losses associated with the use of a long-lived asset (asset group)**
> f. A current expectation that, more likely than not, a long-lived asset (asset group) will be sold or otherwise disposed of significantly before the end of its previously estimated useful life. The term *more likely than not* refers to a level of likelihood that is more than 50 percent

The most useful indicator, of course, is (e) above. There is no known index that can adjust costs, or values, downward to reflect negative operating conditions. Yet many companies do have loss operations, which can be either temporary or permanent.

Permanent operating losses are a virtually certain indicator that the carrying amounts of assets are too high. Comparing operating losses to assets whose dollar amounts have been increased because of indexing will almost universally suggest that the assessment is way too high; such assessments absolutely do not reflect current FMV.

Keep in mind that the standard for *all* property taxes has to be, and is, FMV; FMV directly implies that the assets could be sold for that amount to the proverbial "willing buyer." But if the assets are generating losses, instead of a profit, then there will be no willing buyers at the amount of the assessment.

By definition, when there are operating losses which are expected to continue, one can reliably expect that assessments are overstated.

It is a principle of valuation that *there has to be economic support for any value.* If an asset will generate $100,000 of net income, and investors require a 10% return on investment, then the assets supporting the income cannot be worth more than $1 million.

There are two variables in this equation that have to be looked at: the income projection and the required rate of return. If the assumptions are supportable and any reasonable observer would agree that the two assumptions above were correct there is a *prima facie* case for a reduction in the carrying amount of the assets to $1 million.

This necessary reduction in assessed value would be irrespective of what the original cost was, the depreciated original cost, or an assessors indexing of original cost. With an income of $100,000 and a 10% rate of return the only answer as to the FMV of the underlying assets is $1 million. There obviously is a false sense of precision about this number and this approach; the real answer should probably be stated as $1 million ±10%.

Assuming now that the company has a loss operation, and the assessor shows her value for the property at perhaps $2.5 million, it is time for an appeal. Inasmuch as the appeal procedures are not identical locality to locality, all we can do here is provide a generalized outline. Step one, of course, is to discuss this with the assessor, show her the facts, and ask for a reduction. If that does not work there is usually an appeals board to which differences of opinion between the taxpayer and the assessor are brought. The members of this board are usually local citizens who do not necessarily have valuation expertise.

If the appeals board, in turn, rejects the request for an assessment reduction the next, and usually final, step is to go to court, arguing that the local assessor has not complied with her state's statutes or controlling court cases. Inasmuch as "value" in the final analysis is a matter of judgment, there may not be a court case directly on point, and the statute may not have been drafted to cover your specific fact pattern.

It is then necessary for the company to hire an appraiser, working with a local attorney, to develop a supportable basis for the lower value. These reports, and the author has been involved explicitly in this exact type of case, have to demonstrate conclusively:

- The present value of the anticipated cash flows
- The discount rate that "willing buyers" would utilize

Then in addition to a discounted cash flow (DCF) analysis, it is very helpful if the valuation specialist is able to locate more or less comparable sales. This' will demonstrate that actual transactions—between buyers and sellers—have resulted in supportable market values equivalent to the value indication developed from the DCF approach.

A well-supported valuation report submitted by the taxpayer probably will prevail. Most tax jurisdictions have neither comparable expertise in-house nor the resources to hire an equally competent valuation specialist to take the opposite position. As a note, in many high-income divorce cases both parties can and do hire separate valuation specialists and then it is up to a judge to decide between the competing appraisal reports. Property tax appeals do not often have competing appraisals. The taxpayer does have a slight disadvantage inasmuch as the local judge may have a slight leaning to maintaining the jurisdiction's tax revenues, "all other things being equal."

Temporary operating losses are much harder for a company to handle. The reason is that projections of future operating results, on which DCF analyses are made, would show future positive earnings and presumably positive cash flows once the losses are turned around. Nonetheless, if the reduction is expected to continue for two or more years, it would pay to request an adjustment, even for a short time.

The reduced short-term earnings potential will reduce the value of the assets at that point in time. "Value" is always at a specific date, often January 1st for property taxes. If the current year's losses are material, then it would be worthwhile to at least discuss the current position with the assessor, indicating if things improve in one year, or two years at the outside, that you would then tell them and expect the assessed value to be restored.

There is an aphorism among bank lending officers, "I can take bad news, but I can't take surprises!" The same holds true for assessors. They understand losses occur and such losses affect the FMV of company assets. A temporary reduction in assessed value, and hence property taxes for the year, is easier to swallow if the government officials realize that as soon as things turn around you will "play ball" with them.

The question may be raised at this point, "How much should a short-term loss be to request a reduction is assessment?" No generalized answer is possible, other than to say materiality should govern. Typically, company tax officials have a lot to do, and fighting a one-year or two-year assessment reduction may not appear to have too high a priority. If you have an assessor who has been "reasonable" in the past, you should at least ask. If you face a long uphill battle probably it would be better to devote resources elsewhere.

REAL ESTATE TAXES AND APPEALS

Many of the problems, and opportunities, discussed above for personal property do not apply to valuations for real estate taxes, as developed in most jurisdictions. The reason is quite simple.

There are relatively few market transactions for items of personal property. Yes, there are used equipment dealers and auctions in which industrial equipment is bought and sold. But no more than 5% of personal property ever goes through the hands of a used equipment dealer or an industrial auction. Most assets are bought by the original owner, used by him until they wear out or are discarded (often for periods much longer than assumed by depreciation tables) and then replaced. There are few places where assessors can go to obtain accurate current prices for assets in use, so they have to rely on indexes and depreciation tables. Neither assessors, nor companies, can afford to hire skilled valuation specialists to value, or revalue, hard assets on a recurring basis. Some shortcuts have to be taken simply to arrive at an estimate of FMV.

Real estate is different from other hard assets in a major way. There are numerous real estate transactions representing purchases and sales of property. These transactions are recorded so the public (including appraisers and assessors) has access to the data. Most transactions are limited to a small regional geographical area (a county, city, or municipality) and those interested in studying the transactions can literally go and see the property. Obviously, it is impractical for a local assessor to visually inspect machinery and equipment, even if he or she were qualified to determine the current FMV.

But for real estate, essentially the required information is available, and it represents *actual transactions*, usually between "*a willing buyer and a willing seller*." For purposes of this chapter we disregard forced or liquidation sales which usually do not fulfill the definition because there is hardly ever a "willing seller" in such a transaction. Companies and owners do not willingly run their business to enter bankruptcy, so sales in bankruptcy or forced just prior to bankruptcy do not meet the test of FMV. It may be hard at times to distinguish a forced sale from the published data, but a knowledgeable local assessor or appraiser will simply recognize such transactions as part of their professional expertise and experience and then disregard them in any subsequent analysis.

So we essentially have excellent and accurate records of all real estate transactions accessible both to assessors and companies and their hired valuation consultants. These records, in turn, usually reflect true FMV, absent any known problems.

So, how do assessors determine the tax base for real estate? They look at recent sales. In time periods with relatively slow price increases (or, recently, price decreases) it is relatively easy to determine the FMV of a commercial building by reference to recent sales of similar transactions. Appraisers, and assessors, review the characteristics of the subject property being valued, and compare it to the actual transactions which are available. They look at the size of the subject property relative to the size of the comparable sales and adjust up or down for this characteristic. Similar adjustments are made for age, location, zoning, transportation, and so on.

A reader with a single-family home can estimate quite reliably the FMV of her own home. The mental process involves comparing your house to others sold, or offered for sale, in your neighborhood and adjusting for finished basement or swimming pool or larger lot or an extra bath. This thought process is identical with that used by valuation specialists. It is a basic premise of valuation that there are never, well almost never, truly comparable, much less identical properties. Adjustments almost *always* have to be made, and it is in the ability to make these adjustments that professional valuation specialists apply their knowledge.

To get back to the subject of tax values for commercial and industrial real estate, the real valuation problems revolve around how many "comparable" property sales can be identified. How many adjustments have to be made to relate the actual sale price of a different property to yours? When sales are few, and prices have moved substantially since the last sale it is quite difficult to develop a truly supportable value, one that will stand up to close scrutiny.

CFOs (chief financial officers) and controllers who are concerned about the assessment of their company's real estate should follow this procedure:

■ There are not enough resources for assessors, or companies, to determine professionally the exact value of every commercial and industrial property every year. Therefore, it makes sense for companies with substantial real estate holdings to separate their parcels into three categories. In effect, one should conduct "triage" on all holdings. One group obviously is not overvalued and can be put aside. A second category represents parcels where brief scrutiny of the assessed value suggests that the company may be paying excess property tax on the real estate. The third category represents parcels which may be over-assessed.

For the portion that appears overvalued by the local community the following steps may provide opportunity for reducing the tax burden:

Step 1. Compare the current assessment with the net book value of the property. Parcels in this potentially overassessed group will have assessments significantly above net book value (original cost of the land and building less accumulated depreciation on the building).

Step 2. Call a commercial real estate broker in the community and ask for her opinion of the current value of the property in relation to the assessed value. Of course this will be just an opinion, not an appraisal or valuation.

Step 3. Assuming the broker confirms the suspicion that the property is significantly overassessed relative to current market conditions, the next logical step is to call the tax assessor and ask for their basis of valuation. They have to tell you how they arrived at their estimate of value. Often the answer will be that the assigned value had been derived by application of a building cost index. Certainly, such a valuation approach will overvalue the current FMV.

Step 4. By calling the perceived discrepancy to the attention of the assessor this gives them a chance to adjust the valuation on an informal basis.

Step 5. Assuming the assessor, however, asserts "my valuation is correct and I am not going to change it" the next step is the formal appeal process.

Step 6. Virtually every community has state-mandated processes for hearing taxpayer appeals.

Step 7. The company itself can do sufficient work to develop a "case" that the property is worth less than the assessed value. It may be necessary to enlist the aid of a local commercial real estate broker at this point and pay her for a good list of comparable sales and obvious adjustments. Such a broker should be compensated for her time, but at this stage it will be apparent to the company that a reduction in assessment will more than pay for the cost of the appeal, when one considers that a reduction in assessment this year will provide continuing savings in the future.

Step 8. Now, if the appeal fails and the company is convinced that the FMV is substantially less than the assessment the final step is to go to court.

Step 9. This involves retaining a local real estate attorney and obtaining a formal appraisal from a qualified appraiser, often a "MAI" which is the professional designation (**M**ember of the **A**ppraisal **I**nstitute) of real estate appraisers.

"CONTINGENCY" CONSULTANTS

CFOs and controllers should keep one thing in mind. There are a lot of "consultants" who will promise to appeal tax assessments in exchange for a percentage of the "savings" and these "savings" may extend over several years. On the surface this seems like a good deal. The company has no out-of-pocket costs up front and the consultants only get paid if the company wins. Does this sound like accident lawyers and class action lawyers? The answer is yes.

There is nothing wrong in hiring an attorney on a contingency basis but . . . professional valuation specialists cannot, and do not, work on a contingency. The reason is crystal clear upon reflection: Valuation requires professional judgment, applied objectively. A lawyer is hired by a client to represent him; everyone knows that his loyalty is to the client, not some sort of objective "truth."

Because valuation requires objective judgment it would be virtually impossible for an appraiser's pay to be determined on the value he proposes. Contingency payments are usually a fixed percentage of the amounts won, as an injury lawyer may receive 33% of whatever damages are awarded to his client by a jury. The higher the payout, the higher will be his compensation. Of course the attorney for the other side also has a motivation to win, albeit maybe not on a percentage basis.

But in terms of valuation, how can an appraiser get up on the witness stand, swear to "tell the truth, the whole truth and nothing but the truth" when his expected compensation, even whether he gets paid or not, hangs in the balance? If his compensation is a function of his valuation, it is very hard to assert than one is not motivated by the opportunity to win. Further, the lower the value the more he would be paid! Who would believe the valuation specialist? The alternative is for each side to hire their own appraiser, which often happens in a divorce, and then the two appraisers choose a third. But even that third appraiser could not work on a contingency basis and remain objective.

In short, be wary of any valuation specialist who holds himself out as willing to work on a contingency. If you hire such a person, do not be surprised if his "values" are successfully challenged.

The bottom line, if you are going to court to challenge an assessment you *can* hire a contingency attorney, but you should *not* hire an appraiser on a contingency basis. Thus, any appeal will cost the company at a minimum for out of pocket valuation costs, so the chances of winning, and the amount of a potential reduction in assessed value, has to be weighed against the chances of prevailing.

The author's firm does not take contingency work, so our views may be somewhat biased. Having said that, if you have a good case, go for it. If the case is weak, do you really want to expend your time, and antagonize the assessor, for the chance of a small win?

 ## SUMMARY

Property tax assessments, because of the large number of taxpayers, have been computerized in most tax jurisdiction. Indexes are applied to the original cost of the asset as they were reported to the tax authorities in the year of acquisition. Indexes have their place for "normal" changes in condition and price levels.

If a company has a facility that is losing money, there is no known index that can identify this or determine the true current FMV. Depending on the dollar amounts involved, the company should first discuss the assessment with the taxing authorities. Only if satisfaction is not received should the company go to court. Going to court involves legal and valuation fees, but often the potential savings in property tax will more than pay for the time and effort.

 ## NOTE

1. The term *ad valorem* is derived from the Latin *ad valentiam*, meaning "to the value." It is commonly applied to a tax imposed on the value of property. Real property taxes that are imposed by the states, counties, and cities are the most common type of *ad valorem* taxes. *ad valorem* taxes can, however, be imposed on personal property. For example, a motor vehicle tax may be imposed on personal property such as an automobile www.thefreedictionary.com.

CHAPTER TWELVE

Developing the Fair Value of Fixed Assets

T RADITIONALLY, BOTH ACCOUNTING FOR and control of fixed assets has been based on the *cost* to the company of the asset. Assets are recorded at cost when acquired, depreciated down to salvage value, or to zero, and then removed from the fixed-asset register, or property record, upon sale or other disposition. Very straight-forward, with the possible exception that an impairment charge may have to be taken in situations where the economic value is severely impacted. As discussed in Chapter 5 on Impairment there are some clear indicators as to when assets must be tested. In the absence of any such indicators, the original cost of the asset continues to be utilized for both accounting and internal control. Insurance and property tax assessments also usually start with the original cost.

Original cost can either be the amount paid to the vendor (including freight and installation) or an allocated portion of the purchase price in a business combination. In a business combination the new "cost" is based on the "fair value" of the asset at the time of the transaction. Many companies, in a business combination, will have retained a valuation firm to determine the fair value of the Property, Plant, and Equipment (PP&E), working capital, and intangible assets, with goodwill as the balancing item.

From the perspective of internal control, there is no difference between acquiring a new asset directly from its vendor, and acquiring the same asset as part of an acquisition of a target company. Once the asset is placed in service, with its own property identifier, and it appears on the property record, the "cost" of the asset is solely a matter of historical interest. True control of an asset does not depend on its original cost, or its current depreciated amount (original cost less accumulated depreciation).

Accounting under generally accepted accounting principles (GAAP) has traditionally precluded writing up the value of assets; under GAAP one only writes *down* assets through an impairment charge following unusual circumstances. This long-standing state of affairs may well change as advocates of fair value accounting push for a new paradigm.

WHAT IS THE FAIR VALUE OF PROPERTY, PLANT, AND EQUIPMENT?

The definition of fair value adopted by the Financial Accounting Standards Board (FASB) and the International Accounting Standards Board (IASB) has two unfortunate characteristics that make its use for purposes of valuing PP&E very difficult. The definition of fair value was really written for valuing financial instruments. As currently written, fair value is: (1) what an asset could be sold for; and (2) what a "market participant" would pay to buy the asset.

Apply that test to a financial instrument, say a bond issued by a smaller publicly traded company. You would first find the "market participants" among a group of investment and banking institutions, say Merrill Lynch and Goldman Sachs. You would then call them up, tell them the full description of your security, and they would quote you a bid and an ask price, which might be very close to each other. The fair value of the security would then be determined by what Merrill and Goldman were offering you on the valuation date for that security.

This concept of fair value works very well indeed for financial instruments for which there is a reasonably active market, at least two or three dealers who make a market in that type of security. Further, if one has a portfolio of securities, it is entirely feasible to remove a single security from the total portfolio and sell it. Instead of the security, you now have cash; the value of the portfolio has not changed—except perhaps for very nominal transaction costs.

Looked at in a slightly different way, every security within a portfolio stands on its own. The value of a single security in a portfolio is not affected by any other securities held, any securities formerly held or any securities that could be bought in the future. Thus, the value of a portfolio of investment securities is essentially the sum of the values of whatever securities make up the portfolio. The whole is exactly the sum of the parts.

Now let us look at how valuation specialists determine the fair value of PP&E. We often need to develop an indication of fair value for PP&E in an allocation of purchase price in a business combination. Other situations when fair value information is needed are for determining the value of collateral in a borrowing situation, for insurance, and for testing the reasonableness of property tax assessments.

Unfortunately, the FASB's accounting definition of fair value has to be used for financial reporting, but probably cannot be used for valuing collateral, placing insurance, or evaluating property tax assessments. In this chapter we deal only with financial reporting. Separate chapters on Property Tax (Chapter 11) and Insurance (Chapter 10) cover those two areas of control over PP&E on a separate basis. In a borrowing situation, lenders using PP&E as collateral want liquidation values, which invariably are quite low.

For financial reporting of the fair value of PP&E, we are required to use the FASB definition of fair value originally promulgated in the Statement of Financial Accounting Standard (SFAS) 157 and now incorporated into Accounting Standards Codification (ASC) 820. As mentioned before this incorporates what an asset could be sold for to a market participant.

However, PP&E is rarely sold, and certainly not sold piecemeal. The reason is clear. Take an assembly line in a factory or an entire manufacturing plant. Suppose someone gave you, the reader, an assembly line for diesel-electric locomotives but told you that you personally had to run the facility and could not retain or hire any existing or former employees. You would have to hire and train all new employees. Further, all you would have is the production facility and no marketing resources to try and sell the output to actual or prospective customers.

At that point we can ask just how valuable is the assemblage of machinery sitting there? Nobody to run it. Nobody to sell the output. In this admittedly contrived situation the fair value of the assets, and what they could be sold for to a market participant would depend on whether anyone else wanted to be in the diesel-electric locomotive business, an industry with exactly two participants as this is written.

If there were no market for the factory as a whole, then the fair value of the equipment would be what appraisers call liquidation value, which is defined as what the assets would bring in an auction. As a rule of thumb, auction values for used equipment might be 5 to 15% of the cost of new comparable equipment. This refers to somewhat specialized or dedicated assets. Common machine tools such as lathes and milling machines, with multiple potential uses, might bring 25 to 35% depending on age and condition.

Now assume that there is a market participant who would be interested in acquiring the factory, on an "as-is, where-is" basis. How would such a prospective buyer determine the fair value, that is, what the assets might be worth to him; such an analysis puts an upper limit on what he would be willing to pay.

VALUE IN-USE OF PROPERTY, PLANT, AND EQUIPMENT

If there were a prospective buyer interested in getting into the locomotive business *and* willing to buy the existing factory on an as-is, where-is basis, there is one thing he would *not* do or try to do, to set a purchase price. He would *not* determine the value of each piece of equipment on a separate stand-alone basis.

The only basis for valuing the equipment, for determining how much such a market participant would actually pay, is to estimate what *income* could be derived from use of the factory to produce the product, locomotives, for which the plant was designed. But the factory equipment sitting there idle will not produce locomotives, much less sell them.

The prospective investor thus would have to develop an overall business plan, budgeting in costs for labor, management, production inventory, and all aspects of selling, general, and administrative (SG&A) expenses. Further, one would have to estimate future sales and the related working capital requirements. With this financial projection the prospective investor could determine the present value of the anticipated future income that the facility could conceivably generate, allowing for all aspects of business risk.

What we have just described is exactly what valuation specialists do in determining fair value using an income approach. In fact this is probably the most common tool used by appraisers, and is how we tell clients what a business is worth.

But wait. Initially, we were just trying to determine the value of the manufacturing *assets* on the factory floor. But in order to do that we had to develop a business plan and in effect price out that plan.

The message should be clear. By themselves a conglomeration of assets on a factory floor are worth very little without all the other related assets that go to make up a complete functioning operating business. The value of the assets is the income they will produce, and on a stand-alone basis, PP&E assets, by themselves, generate no income or cash flow. Only as part of a broader business, where the assets are a necessary component, but not sufficient by themselves, can the assets be said to have significant value.

The ideas expressed so far are an introduction to a valuation concept that is not necessarily well known, but one that is easily understandable once it is described. Assets can be valued in-exchange, or in-use. Value in-exchange is what the items would bring on a stand-alone basis. For PP&E a stand-alone basis might or might not include working capital, a building, and in certain circumstances even incorporate a workforce. To distinguish a value in-exchange of assets, from the value in-use of the business as a going concern, we look to potential alternate uses that may differ from the original purpose of the assemblage.

If in practice the "highest and best use" of assets is as part of a going concern, we are now in the realm of value in-use. Ordinarily, value in-use is greater than the value in-exchange for PP&E. A word of warning, however, financial instruments, securities, are always valued on an in-exchange basis. FASB and IASB always first think of fair value in the concept of value in-exchange to market participants. This is in contrast to the value in-use of assets to the firm that actually has plans and resources to put the PP&E to work.

In fact, GAAP and International Financial Reporting Standards (IFRS) seemingly are prejudiced *against* value in-use because they maintain that the value is "entity specific," and not based on some one or more unknown market participants. If I am already in the heavy equipment manufacturing business I will be able to pay for the assemblage of assets designed to produce locomotives. Were I to be valuing the same assets for an advertising agency (or other professional service business), to the contrary, the assets would have little more than liquidation value. This disparity of value, depending on who is the prospective user, is what troubles the accounting regulators.

Yet this disparity which troubles regulators, the fact that the same asset can have differing values depending on circumstances, is the real world that valuation specialists and their clients inhabit. The theoretical world of perfect markets for financial instruments does not work for PP&E and as far as intangible assets are concerned, there usually is *NO* market.

WHAT WOULD HAPPEN IF FAIR VALUE REPORTING FOR PROPERTY, PLANT, AND EQUIPMENT WAS REQUIRED?

There is a real question as to just what the fair value of PP&E on a company balance sheet would mean. For the most part, PP&E is not for sale, unlike financial instruments which can be sold without affecting the basic business model. But if any manufacturer were to try and sell a portion of its PP&E, what would happen to overall production and revenue?

Could an auto company like Volkswagen sell its assembly plants? Who would buy them? What could another buyer, other than a competitor, another auto company, do with an assembly plant? The only conceivable buyers, irrespective of whether fair value is above or below book value, are competitors. And competitors are likely to be feeling the same economic conditions as the subject firm as well as owning and operating similar facilities. In other words the value in-use to the owner is likely to be the value in-exchange if there are other actual or potential buyers.

Another way to look at this is to ask, just how would a shareholder or security analyst make better investment decisions were the fair value of PP&E to be developed and disclosed? While financial instruments can be sold individually or in total and not affect the basic business model of a company, selling or disposing of any material part of productive equipment will in and of itself change the basic nature of the company.

Suppose you own shares in a small publicly traded company, where PP&E makes up say 20% of total assets, and management tells you that the fair value of the PP&E is 5% above book value. What would you want management to do? What should you do as an investor?

The truth is that as an investor you have two choices. Hold your investment or sell your investment. It is hard to see how knowing the fair value of PP&E is going to aid you in that determination. Is it a good sign that fair value is above book value, or perhaps is it a bad sign? Yet there are many people who strongly support the idea that companies should develop and disclose the fair value of all assets, including PP&E.

 ## CONNECTION BETWEEN FAIR VALUE AND BOOK VALUE

The book value of assets is simply the original cost of the asset, less the sum of depreciation charges to date. Assuming the original purchase price as recorded was representative of the market at the time of acquisition, then the book value today is a function of depreciation charges. As discussed in Chapter 4 companies almost invariably depreciate assets more rapidly than any diminution in utility or economic value; the result is that book values at any point in time may be too low, relative to the real fair value.

Companies frequently choose tax depreciation and lives as the basis for computing financial depreciation. As mentioned, tax lives and depreciation methods are set by Congress and the Internal Revenue Service (IRS) in an effort to stimulate investment. The easiest way to do this is to allow companies to use accelerated depreciation methods and unduly short lives. This political policy decision reached its zenith in proposals to allow 100% depreciation in the year of acquisition, which in small measure is already incorporated into the Internal Revenue Code.

Would anyone suggest that financial reports would be more useful if all PP&E were written off to expense the same year they were acquired? Depreciation is supposed to reflect, in some measure, the decline in value over time of long-lived assets. Using too short a life, or too accelerated a method (the ultimate of course is 100% expensing as mentioned) means that at any point book value is likely to be less than fair value. Overly rapid depreciation charges, and too much accumulated depreciation, mean that net book value (cost less accumulated depreciation) is too low, which in turn means that fair value will likely be higher than book value.

This idea, supported by more than 40 years experience, is sometimes hard for people to accept. The difficulty arises because most people think of depreciation in terms of automobiles and personal computers. Automobiles, at the retail level, decrease in value very quickly. Sometimes it is said that a car loses 20% of its value just being driven out of the dealer's lot. With respect to personal computers how many people are still using computers that are more than three or four years old? The replacement cycles of personal computers seemingly never ends and the market value of a three-year-old computer probably is less than 10% of its original cost. The same could be said of television sets, but very few people sell or trade in a television set so the real market value of a used set is not readily available. But for personal computers and cars almost every reader has a pretty good idea of current values, and those values are way below original cost.

What is true for personal computers and automobiles, however, is *not* necessarily true of production equipment or buildings. Have you ever heard of a company "trading in" a warehouse because the "current model" is obsolete? Warehouses last a very long time. Similarly, a bottling line in a factory is designed for long life, and hardly ever wears out or has to be replaced with a new model.

The tremendous growth in productivity in the United States in large measure is due to the major capital expenditures that most companies make. The vast majority of those expenditures are *not* in personal computers or cars, but in assets with very long effective lives.

Consequently, when companies determine effective lives for financial reporting that are based on tax lives and depreciation methods, they highly understate current values. Then, when the fair value of PP&E is determined objectively by valuation specialists, the value obtained more often than not is higher than the book value. Is this a real gain, or just recognition of overly aggressive ("conservative") expensing?

Appraisers are often retained to determine the fair value of PP&E, for example, in a purchase price allocation. What we typically find is that the total fair value is surprisingly close to the book value. This congruence is actually the sum of two disparate phenomena. First, as discussed before, is the fact that book depreciation is almost always too fast, influenced as it is by tax policy. Going in the other direction are assets on the property register that simply cannot be found, missing for one of a number of reasons. Finally, of course, there are fully depreciated assets with no book value that are still in place and still in use. These assets have value for insurance, perhaps for property tax assessment and certainly for any internal return on invested capital calculations.

 ## WHAT WOULD INVESTORS LEARN FROM FAIR VALUE DISCLOSURES OF PROPERTY, PLANT, AND EQUIPMENT?

In the final analysis, the only way to determine the fair value of PP&E is to estimate the income that the assets will produce in the future. Thus an ultra-modern factory equipped with state-of-the art machinery and tooling to produce hula-hoops might only be worth auction value for the equipment because few investors would expect substantial future cash flows from the sale of hula-hoops.

Now assume that the owner of the hula-hoop factory is required to develop and report publicly the fair value of the PP&E, the machinery, equipment, and tooling. Estimating the present value of future cash flows will lead to a low number, so low that the liquidation value may be higher. In either event, the financial statements of the manufacturer will show a huge impairment loss from the new equipment cost entailed in constructing such a state-of-the-art plant.

But under today's accounting, whenever there is an impairment loss, companies already must disclose this and make the appropriate charge to earnings to reflect the diminution in value. So, when there is a massive downturn in the economy, then any sort of fair value accounting requirement will accomplish nothing that is not already known.

Okay, let us take a different example, a facility to produce original equip-ment manufacturer (OEM) auto parts for the major automobile manufacturers. Certainly one would expect a combination of old and new equipment and tooling in an auto parts plant; the current book value—based on original cost depreciated to date of today's equipment—will *not* reflect current fair value.

This is just the type of example used by fair value proponents. They say, "Shouldn't shareholders and creditors be informed about today's fair value of the factory and its equipment?" The proponents uniformly answer that rhetorical question of their own in the affirmative, without necessarily answer-ing the more meaningful question, "How could we *use* the new fair value information to make better investing decisions?"

Before answering how any fair value information could be used, let us look one step down as to how the company itself, or its valuation consultants, would determine the fair value of the PP&E. Based on the discussion earlier in this chapter, the valuation consultant would ask management for its best projec-tions of future sales, future capital expenditures and anticipated margins (low) for anticipated sales to the major auto companies. With a relatively simple discounted cash flow (DCF) analysis, the fair value of the plant, for anticipated future use for parts manufacturing, is going to be a direct function of future sales and profits.

In other words, the fair value of the equipment is not going to be derived from the specific pieces of equipment; rather, the fair value is based on future sales and profits. If the outlook for automobile sales is rosy, and OEM parts sales will be rising and with good margins, the reported fair value is going to be high and increasing, compared to prior reports. By the same token, if the outlook for autos is gloomy, the fair value based on a DCF analysis will be low and diminishing from prior reports.

The fair value of machinery and equipment used in an ongoing production process has value only to the extent that future output can be sold profitably. But as that profitability increases, so will the fair value increase, almost in lockstep.

What will happen is that as the economic outlook brightens, the company would, under fair value accounting, report increased fair values of its PP&E; that increment of value could favorably affect investor perceptions just when things already look good. Conversely, if the sales outlook is bleak the reported fair value would have to decrease, resulting in an impairment charge just when things already look bad.

What we will have then is that the reported fair value of PP&E will appear to go up in good times, and go down in bad times. You might think, "So what, that's just what we would expect." But then how do we answer the question, "What *new* information is being provided by the company to investors as a result of the fair value disclosures?"

In the author's opinion this is where the fair value proposals for periodic reporting of PP&E totally break down. Investors already know when the automobile business is doing well, and when it is going down. A company will have no information about future economic conditions in a major industry that is not already available to investors. Put a different way, fair value disclosures by companies regarding their PP&E will only reinforce existing understanding; it will *not* shed new light or provide incremental knowledge.

Meanwhile, since there is no "Free Lunch," the cost to a company of developing, auditing, and reporting the fair value of PP&E would add non-value-added cost to the system as a whole, while producing little if any net benefit. We should say here, in the interest of full disclosure, that if fair value information of PP&E is required, it will certainly favor those of us already in the valuation business. Trying to be impartial and objective, however, leads this valuation specialist to the conclusion that demanding the fair value of PP&E is not in the best interest of the total economy.

 ## SUMMARY

Both the FASB and IASB have indicated that their long-run goal is to have financial reporting on a fair value basis. This would presumably include companies being required to determine the fair value for all of its PP&E.

The problem is that the definition of fair value used by standard setters deals with value in-exchange, not value in-use. Yet the value in-exchange for PP&E is essentially going to be liquidation or auction value unless the determination is based on the income the PP&E can generate. But if companies determine the value in-use based on anticipated future income, readers of financial statements will not receive useful information.

When the economy is doing well, increased value will be reported, and when the economy is doing poorly, those same PP&E items will be shown to have lost value. But investors and creditors already know this, so the incremental value of forcing companies to undergo the cost of developing fair value information will be very slight, if it even provides any benefit at all.

CHAPTER THIRTEEN

Control of Fixed Assets under International Financial Reporting Standards

THE INITIAL RECOGNITION AND measurement of Property, Plant, and Equipment (PP&E) is generally the same under International Financial Reporting Standards (IFRS) as it is in the United States under generally accepted accounting principles (GAAP). Assets to be capitalized must have future benefit to the firm, and must be reliably measurable. Equipment required to meet legal and environmental regulations, even though it may not generate specific cash flows or direct future benefit, can still be capitalized because without them other assets could not be used.

According to a recent book[1] the initial capitalized cost for IFRS includes:

- Purchase Price
- Purchase taxes, including duty
- Less supplier discounts and rebates
- Transportation inbound
- Installation and assembly

Ordinarily the cash price paid is the cost, but in the case of an exchange, the transaction is to be measured at fair value of the acquired asset or the net book value of the asset(s) given up. If any government grants are involved, reducing the net cost to the acquirer, only the reduced net amount can be capitalized.

IFRS permits expensing of items under a certain minimum amount, similar to what GAAP permits and we recommend in this book.

Essentially, the IFRS rules parallel those of U.S. GAAP. At this point using the barebones definition, there are few practical differences between accounting for PP&E as between GAAP and IFRS. But here is where significant changes start to appear.

There are two major differences under IFRS. First, component depreciation is *required*. Second, with certain limitations, companies are permitted to *revalue* PP&E.

COMPONENT DEPRECIATION

This topic is covered in Chapter 14 and for those just dealing with IFRS issues we repeat conceptually some of what is discussed there. In the United States we recommended cost segregation as a means of speeding up depreciation expense for taxes, thus providing a present value benefit for the cash flows that are involved. In the United States the cost segregation methodology and approach is functionally equivalent to the IFRS's "component depreciation." In the United States, for tax purposes, componentization is essentially limited to *buildings*, and not generally used for financial reporting. In IFRS the rules specify that whenever the components of a larger asset have differing lives, each component must be set up as a separate asset and depreciated separately. Thus, the IFRS rules apply for financial reporting to major pieces of machinery and equipment, as well as buildings.

For U.S. taxes, component depreciation speeds up the timing of depreciation expense for determining taxable income. The greater the depreciation expense recognized earlier, the greater will be the present value of cash flow due to taxes being paid later. Component depreciation does not provide a total increase in depreciation. What it does is speed up the deduction, so on a time value of money basis, the earlier you can claim depreciation expense, the sooner you get the benefit of the depreciation.

However, it must always be remembered that at the end of the asset's life, the total deductions for depreciation remains the same; it is only the timing that changes. But if a company has a ten percent cost of capital, getting a deduction in year three is markedly better than taking that same deduction in year 33.

In U.S. tax accounting, by separating out major components of a building, one can get substantial savings. The biggest savings can come from an analysis of the electrical system and components, followed by land improvements, millwork, finishes, plumbing, and heating, ventilation, and air conditioning (HVAC). Getting a 15-year life for land improvements is better than a 39-year life for the total building.

Under U.S. GAAP, there is no requirement that the component depreciation taken for taxes be used to financial reporting, other than for the impact of timing differences on deferred tax assets and liabilities. One does not have to depreciate electrical components for financial reporting based on the schedule determined for tax return purposes.

In IFRS, however, component depreciation is mandatory for financial reporting, irrespective of what a company does for its tax returns. This concept of component depreciation for financial reporting at one time was proposed in the United States by the American Institute of Certified Public Accountants (AICPA). However, there was concerted push-back from companies and the proposal went nowhere.

The reason was simple. Not only was there potentially significant cost involved in "carving up" a single total cost from the contractor to arrive at the component depreciation. There would be substantial additional expense in the property record system. Instead of a single line item for "Building at 1000 Main St. . . . $2,000,000," there might have to be ten or more separate line items in the property register for each component, with its own separate life.

Remember, earlier in the book we recommended having as high as possible a minimum capitalization level. This was to reduce the number of assets being controlled; in turn this reduced effort in the accounting department and made it easier to control the truly important assets. Component depreciation for financial reporting goes in the opposite direction, adding complexity.

On a theoretical basis, component depreciation is preferable to a single life assigned to the total building. Elements of an HVAC or plumbing system undoubtedly will need to be replaced long before the foundation or the structural steel has worn out. If depreciation expense and charges are supposed to reflect diminution in value, the concept of component depreciation makes sense. Some parts of a building do wear out faster than others and one can argue that financial reporting should follow the economics and physical life.

Relatively few U.S. companies have used component depreciation for taxes, and virtually none use it for financial reporting. This is the reason for the pushback against the U.S. proposal several years ago.

If IFRS is adopted in the United States then component depreciation will be mandatory for financial reporting. Companies might as well use it then for taxes and get the cash flow benefits that component depreciation does provide. So it will be perceived as a "two-edged sword" favorable on taxes and unfavorable on financial reporting.

There is, however, a further impact. In the U.S. component depreciation is used almost exclusively for buildings, with the construction cost of buildings deconstructed to maximize tax benefits. But in IFRS the concept is based on "proper" reflection of anticipated lives and economics, not only for buildings but for machinery and equipment.

The implications are clear. If you buy a complex numerically controlled milling machine, you might have to assign separate amounts, and lives, to the software, the computer, the electrical hook-up, and the foundation. This could easily double the size of any property record, and make it much more difficult to control the asset(s). Further, it is not clear whether the Internal Revenue Code, and IRS interpretations, would permit component depreciation for machinery and equipment.

Keep in mind that internal control requires periodic verification that assets are still there and in use. It is relatively easy to assign a single radio frequency identification (RFID) property tag to a $500,000 machine tool and then take an inventory of all RFID tags once every three years or even once every year. But if you have to break down the machine tool, where do you put the tag for the software? How do you identify the foundation separate from the machine itself?

These may only be "straw men" arguments against component depreciation, but depending on company policy, and auditor involvement, there is no question that costs will increase if and when IFRS component depreciation becomes mandatory. One can argue that the financial reporting will be more accurate and will more closely reflect real-world economics. But the fact is that the present U.S. system seems to have been working pretty well for most companies for as long as internal control and auditor involvement has taken place (i.e., since the 1930s!).

Mandatory adoption of component depreciation for buildings and machinery and equipment will be seen as costly, and arguments will be heard that change to practice is being forced on U.S. companies simply for the sake of conforming to IFRS (i.e., what the French want us to do). Do we really want the French determining our financial reporting requirements? Many will argue in the negative.

The advantage, of course, to mandatory component depreciation will come in the tax benefits, but at the expense of more bookkeeping, more auditing, and higher operating expenses. There probably would be a net benefit, but the problem is that the costs will be all too visible, and the benefits hard to tease out of an overall tax provision.

ASSET REVALUATION

When the author was studying accounting, back in the pre-computer era, there were a couple of mantras that were taken as gospel. One of them was:

> "Take your losses immediately but don't recognize gains until the asset is sold."

The reason for this was simple, and intuitive. There are enough uncertainties in business that until cash is realized you do not really know if you have a gain or not. Further, if one could recognize gains—income that is—simply by a stroke of the pen through writing up a journal voucher, the potential for manipulation might be hard to resist.

Yet, this is what is permitted/required under IFRS. The ability to write up assets, in the absence of a sale, may well be one of the greatest changes if the United States were to adopt IFRS. That this is likely to happen is supported by a recent addition by Financial Accounting Standards Board (FASB) to their agenda wherein the Board is contemplating permitting in the United States a rule for investment property comparable to what exists in IFRS. Here is the relevant paragraph (¶31 of International Accounting Standards (IAS) 16) governing asset write-up in IFRS:

> "After recognition as an asset, an item of property, plant, and equipment whose fair value can be measured reliably shall be carried at a revalued amount, being its fair value at the date of the revaluation less any subsequent accumulated depreciation and subsequent accumulated impairment losses. Revaluations shall be made with sufficient regularity to ensure that the carrying amount does not differ materially from that which would be determined using fair value at the end of the reporting period."

Reading these words, the key phrase is "whose fair value can be measured reliably." Inasmuch as valuation specialists determine the fair value of PP&E in

(1) every purchase price allocation; (2) in every property tax appeal; and (3) in every valuation of security as collateral for a loan, it would be hard to argue that PP&E cannot be "measured reliably."

The problem for appraisers, auditors, and of course corporate financial officers is that the fair value of an asset for allocation of a purchase price may differ from fair value for property tax appeal as well as the fair value of the same asset used as collateral. Finally, the value of that specific asset for placement of insurance and proof of loss is still a different amount. This problem of valuing PP&E is covered in Chapter 12.

Keep in mind that even if the same set of assumptions is made by two different appraisers, the fair value determination will likely only be within 10% of each other. So there are really two separate problems in asset revaluation. First, what is the "correct" fair value of the asset? The second problem is that even if everyone agrees on the proper premise of value, valuation simply is not that precise!

Every appraiser will agree, at least in an informal setting after a drink or two that two equally competent appraisers are likely to come up with somewhat different answers. The degree of precision will most likely be plus or minus ten percent. Specifically, therefore, if a company obtains a fair value estimate from an outside valuation specialist, and then for whatever reason gets a second opinion, it is almost certain that the second appraiser's values will not be identical with the first. Remember, if you contact two different realtors to put your house on the market, you are likely to get two different estimates of what the house could be sold for.

Valuation is reliable, but only within certain parameters. It simply is not possible to get two independent appraisers to come up with identical answers. Each will have a range, and the two ranges undoubtedly will overlap, but in accounting we cannot book a range, we must use a specific dollar amount. As many valuation specialists have expressed it, "valuation is not an exact science."

Now if a company revalues PP&E one year, and then two or three years later has to undertake a new valuation, but it is by a different appraiser, the potential for a substantial increase, or decrease, in value is obvious. In any year, a 10% swing in the fair value of PP&E could double, or cut in half, the reported earnings for most companies. Is this the kind of variability in income that CFOs (chief financial officers), and investors, are looking for?

IAS 16 goes on to say that PP&E used as part of a continuing business may have to be valued using an income or a depreciated replacement cost approach.

Without going into excruciating nuances of valuation theory, suffice it to say that an income approach applied to PP&E will show *increased* values when business is good, and profits are growing, and will show *decreased* profits when business slows and income is down.

In a word, the IAS 16 approach, if utilized in the United States, will magnify swings in income and reported values. Accelerated growth in good times and accelerated declines in poor times may not be what the proponents of fair value accounting have in mind.

Of course, as a sidebar, the determination of the fair value of a liability, say bonds outstanding, will go down as the company's debt rating goes down and vice versa. So if a company is not doing well and is downgraded by Moody's and S&P the company will show a *gain*! Then when conditions improve and the old credit rating is restored upward, the company will have to show a loss. Just try to explain this to someone who is not an accounting geek.

Now one may question, if these problems exist with IAS 16, why have the problems not showed up in countries that already use IFRS. The answer is pretty clear that most companies have *not* taken advantage of or utilized the ability to choose a revaluation model, keeping in mind that it is a choice, not a requirement.

So one might argue that if existing countries are not burdened with accelerated gains and losses, why should we worry in the United States? The reason that U.S. companies might well take advantage of the revaluation model, even if it has not happened elsewhere, is the compensation policies common in U.S. firms. If management is going to be rewarded for meeting or beating estimates, and revaluing assets would permit such a gain, then at least some companies might be tempted to "choose" revaluation in an otherwise down, or even level year.

Keep in mind that the first time the revaluation model is applied, values certainly will be increased from the date of the assets' acquisition. So, even in a down year, substantial revaluation "profits" can be recognized. Worse, once one company in an industry adopts a revaluation model, it is highly likely that security analysts, in the interest of "true comparability," will request other companies to do the same thing.

Now we can get into all sorts of discussions about measuring income for compensation, and comparing two similarly situated companies. The fact remains that "Gresham's Law of Accounting" (bad accounting drives out good accounting) suggests that few companies want to be left out if their direct competitors do something that will increase reported income and net worth. It is very easy to foresee a true "race to the bottom."

INVESTMENT PROPERTY

IFRS distinguishes between land and buildings owned and operated by companies for production, warehousing, or offices from so-called investment property, which is defined in IAS 40 as:

> "Property (land or a building—or part of a building—or both) held (by the owner or by the lessee under a finance lease) to earn rentals or for capital appreciation or both, rather than for:
>
> a. Use in the production or supply of goods or services or for administrative purposes
> b. Sale in the ordinary course of business"

When first acquired, under IAS 40, investment property is recorded at cost and includes "any directly attributable expenditure." Directly attributable expenditures, likewise, includes professional fees, property transfer taxes, and other transaction costs. But the "cost" does *not* include so-called start-up costs, that is operating losses attained, before achieving a planned level of occupancy and abnormal amounts of wasted material, labor, or other resources incurred in constructing or developing the property. Outside the scope of this book, the International Accounting Standards Board (IASB) recently amended IAS 40 to include leased property and being able to be consider investment property by a lessee.

In requiring that investment property be valued at "fair value" IAS 40 provides a discussion of the determination of fair value that closely approximates what is now in Accounting Standards Codification (ASC) 820, as developed in Statement of Financial Accounting Standard (SFAS) 157. As in U.S. GAAP, the IASB distinguishes fair value from value in-use. The former is based on market conditions and the latter is "entity specific" to the present owner. Disclosure in financial statements has to be fair value, and not value in-use. IAS 40 also provides guidance about a transfer from and to investment property of assets to be used directly by the business. Essentially, the fair value at the time of transfer is to be used.

The major difference between the accounting for investment property and other PP&E used in a business and revalued under IAS 16 is very simple. All changes in the fair value of investment property go directly to the profit and loss statement (P&L), with no upper or lower limits. Under IAS 16's revaluation model, gains for most assets go into other comprehensive income and are accumulated in surplus under the heading of revaluation surplus. If, however, an increase merely reverses a prior decrease or impairment charge, then the increase in fair value can be reflected in current income.

As might be expected, net decreases in fair value under IAS 16, and IAS 40, both go directly to P&L.

The differences between IAS 40 and accounting for real estate investment trusts (REITs) are probably not material, so U.S. adoption of IFRS would not impact REITs. Certainly, as discussed previously, if IFRS were to be adopted in the United States there would be potentially major changes in accounting for PP&E. At a minimum companies would have the option of going to a revaluation model and we predict that this likely would happen.

WHAT IS THE "COST" OF PROPERTY, PLANT, AND EQUIPMENT?

Remember that under IFRS the following costs are to be capitalized as part of the initial cost of acquiring PP&E:

■ Purchase price
■ Purchase taxes, including duty
■ Less supplier discounts and rebates
■ Transportation inbound
■ Installation and assembly

As in GAAP, these costs are included in the initial cost.

When accounting for a business combination, GAAP precludes legal and accounting costs paid by the acquirer. Many observers feel that the investment banking fees, legal, and accounting costs associated with a business combination are similar conceptually to inbound transportation and assembly, in that without them the asset could not be used.

The Financial Accounting Standards Board (FASB) argued that its definition of fair value (ASC 820) when applied to a business combination says that a subsequent buyer would not pay for the original legal, accounting, and investment banker fees. By the same token a company selling a previously installed machine tool will not recover its inbound transportation, installation, and assembly costs, but these latter can be capitalized under both GAAP and IFRS.

If we had to make a prediction, at some point in the future the IASB and FASB will "rationalize" PP&E accounting; companies may not then be able to capitalize transportation, installation, and assembly. Until then, these costs must be capitalized and depreciated subsequently.

 ## SUMMARY

Whether IFRS will be adopted in the United States is an open question as this book is being written. The drumbeat of advocates wishing the United States to join the rest of the world is getting louder and louder, and is being driven by the major accounting firms. That the Big 4 would derive literally billions of dollars of additional consulting and auditing fees when IFRS is adopted here, neither supports nor condemns the concept. It may, however, call into question the objectivity of the loudest proponents.

There are two major differences to accounting as we know it under GAAP. Companies would be required to use component depreciation. This will be costly in certain circumstances, but in the long run may be a good thing in terms of faster tax depreciation and deductions. Perhaps for the first time companies will truly realize that they do not have to use the same lives for books as for taxes, and that tax lives should be chosen to maximize tax deductions, irrespective of what is shown in the GAAP financial statements.

The second major change will be the potential for companies to revalue PP&E and investment property. This will often boost net income and/or net worth. If adopted, it would be a major step toward fair value accounting, the pride and joy of academics and security analysts who think that all the new fair value information will somehow help investors and creditors.

No secrets are disclosed by revealing that more than 40 years of experience in valuation has convinced this appraiser that fair value accounting would be a disaster. This position goes against our self-interest because were fair value to be adopted, our industry's work (and revenue) would more than double. But, it would not provide better information and could easily lead to manipulation, and possibly even outright fraud.

 ## NOTE

1. Nandakumar Ankarath, Salpesh J. Mehta, T.P. Ghosh, and Yass A. Alkafaji, *Understanding IFRS Fundamentals: International Financial Reporting Standards* (New York, NY: John Wiley & Sons, 2010), Chapter 10.

CHAPTER FOURTEEN

Component Depreciation for Buildings*

I N THE UNITED STATES when a company buys a building, say an office, warehouse, or factory the total cost is capitalized. That dollar amount (other than the value of the underlying land) is then depreciated over the useful life assumed for the building.

For federal income tax purposes, most buildings are assigned a 39-year life; accountants by and large use that same 39-year time period for book depreciation as well as taxes. If nothing else, this use of the same life for books and taxes effectively eliminates any deferred tax accounting. Further, using a 39-year life seemingly accords with economics; many buildings may face a degree of functional depreciation or economic obsolescence within that time period.

While there are many buildings in use today that were constructed before 1972, this fact alone does not call into question the use of a 39-year life. The reason is that there is an active market in all types of buildings and there is a high probability that within the first 39 years the original owner will sell to a

* The author wishes to thank Chris Hitselberger, Senior Managing Director of C. B. Richard Ellis, for his help with this chapter. I have known him for years first as a colleague at Marshall & Stevens, Inc. and now as one of the country's leading practitioners in Cost Segregation studies.

third party. Under any type of accounting the new owner of an existing building would start depreciating it based on the cost to the new owner and the expected life to that new owner. Perhaps for simplicity, or from habit, second owners usually also assign their own 39-year life.

INTERNATIONAL FINANCIAL REPORTING STANDARDS HAS A DIFFERENT APPROACH

International Accounting Standards (IAS) have quite a different approach to the depreciation of buildings. As stated in ¶ 43 of IAS 16:

> "Each part of an item of property, plant, and equipment with a cost that is significant in relation to the total cost of the item *shall* be depreciated separately."

Put in plain English, it requires that companies who comply with International Financial Reporting Standards (IFRS):

- Must set up each component of a building as a separate asset
- Depreciate each component separately
- Using a separate estimated life for that specific component

In practice this means that, for example, a company would determine the cost of roofing separately from the cost of the heating, venting, and air conditioning (HVAC) system; it would then assign a specific life to the roof and to the HVAC system and depreciate them separately. Similarly, the cost of special lighting or floor covering, and other items considered personal property, would have to be determined and given its own life.

The IFRS requirements are clear that you are *not* supposed to depreciate a building as a single line item, based on an overall composite weighted life. Each component with an identifying material cost must be treated as a separate line item; depreciation is calculated for that specific category based on its own estimated economic life.

Thus, instead of a single line item entry for a "building," as is now commonly done in the United States, the company sets up perhaps ten or more line items, the total of which of course sum up to the overall building cost. Under IFRS land is originally entered at its cost, as is done in the United States.

At one point there was a proposal by the Accounting Standards Executive Committee (AcSec) of the American Institute of Certified Public

Accountants (AICPA) that U.S. accounting for buildings should be based on individual components, similar to the IFRS model. The AICPA and the Financial Accounting Standards Board (FASB) explored this idea in some detail and subsequently dropped it, based in large part on unfavorable input from many companies. There was fear expressed by the FASB's corporate constituents that a lot of extra work would be entailed in the accounting departments.

Further, the respondents correctly assessed that depreciation expense would be accelerated; as a consequence initial depreciation expense for financial reporting purposes would be accelerated and reported income would be lower. That depreciation is considered a "noncash charge" and is routinely added back to earnings before interest, taxes, depreciation, and amortization (EBITDA) in the quarterly reports to shareholders was either not considered or was disregarded.

For whatever reasons, the FASB dropped the proposal and little has been heard of it since, at least for financial reporting in the United States.

As a side note, as this is written (2011) there is a lot of discussion about possible U.S. adoption of IFRS, or at a minimum permitting U.S. companies to use IFRS instead of GAAP (generally accepted accounting principles). This difference in accounting for PP&E (property, plant, and equipment) is not one of the differences usually discussed but in practice might represent almost as large a change as the IFRS prohibition against last in, first out (LIFO).

 ## COMPONENT DEPRECIATION FOR TAXES

The reason for the digression above on IFRS is simple. Many U.S. taxpayers are *already* utilizing component depreciation for taxes, albeit this is usually under the direction of the tax department. Companies using component depreciation for taxes rarely use it for financial reporting, the usual purview of CFOs (chief financial officers) and controllers.

Sometimes referred to as "cost segregation," this strategy of component depreciation for tax purposes has saved taxpayers, in total, literally billions of dollars. There are really two mysteries here. Why do more companies not use component depreciation or cost segregation for taxes and if they do why do they not use the *same* system for financial reporting?

If any readers have not investigated cost segregation for any buildings they own, the savings from undertaking such a study are guaranteed to provide a huge return on investment (ROI) on the purchase of this book.

So, just what is a "cost seg" study, as it is familiarly called? In its simplest form, a trained professional, one with an engineering and construction background, as well as an understanding of valuation and tax law, decomposes a building into its construction elements. Then a separate life is assigned to each category of asset based on its tax classification under current Internal Revenue Service (IRS) rules. Again, as discussed in Chapter 4 there is no requirement that companies adopting component depreciation for financial reporting would have to use the same lives elsewhere, but if they do adopt the same lives there would be no need for deferred tax accounting.

Cost segregation or component depreciation is not a magic bullet. At the end of 39 years the exact same amount of depreciation will have been taken for taxes and for books as under the simple, "one-size-fits-all" 39-year life. But by taking the depreciation earlier through componentization the time value of money provides a big win for the taxpayer. Exhibit 14.1 shows that, at an assumed 10% cost of capital (the rate that many real estate professionals use) the present value of the tax savings can amount to almost 6% of the building cost.

COMPLYING WITH INTERNAL REVENUE SERVICE REQUIREMENTS

We must stress that while this tax savings is almost invariably found when a cost seg study is performed on a building, a taxpayer cannot simply apply a flat percentage to the total building cost. You must have the study performed because in practice the mix of relative costs of say the HVAC system to the electrical system is going to depend on a number of variables within each building. In other words no two buildings are the same, and each cost seg study *must* be totally specific to that building.

Understanding the contents of Exhibit 14.1 will allow the reader to see how the concepts apply to any building they own. The example assumes a cost of $5 million for the building; the cost of the land would be kept separate and not be part of the analysis.

The valuation specialist will work with the blueprints of the building and separately identify the cost of each item of 5-, 7-, 15-, and 39-year property. We do not show the detailed supporting schedules prepared that identify each type of asset within that life category but they are part of the final cost seg study report prepared for each building.

EXHIBIT 14.1 Cash Flow Benefit from Cost Segregation Study Example

Potential Change in Cash Flow Resulting From a Component Depreciation Study for

Sample

	WITH Component Depreciation Study		WITHOUT Component Depreciation Study	
Property Class	Percentage Assumed	Depreciable Basis	Percentage Assumed	Depreciable Basis
5-Year Property	15%	750,000	0%	0
7-Year Property	2%	100,000	0%	0
15-Year Property	15%	750,000	0%	0
39-Year Property	68%	3,400,000	100%	5,000,000
	Total	$5,000,000	Total	$5,000,000

Tax Basis $5,000,000
Tax Rate 40%
Present Value Factor 10%

Present Value of Changes in Cash Flow

Year 1	First 6 Years	40-Year Life
$72,510	$318,832	$289,526

COMPONENT DEPRECIATION COMPARISON

Year	5 Year	7 Year	15 Year	39 Year	Total Annual Depreciation Expense WITH Study	Total Annual Depreciation Expense W/O Study	Change in Depreciation Expense	After-Tax Change in Cash Flow	Present Value of Changes in Cash Flow
1	150,000	14,286	37,500	43,588	245,374	64,100	181,274	72,510	72,510
2	240,000	24,490	71,250	87,176	422,916	128,200	294,716	117,886	107,169
3	144,000	17,493	64,125	87,176	312,794	128,200	184,594	73,838	61,023
4	86,400	12,495	57,713	87,176	243,784	128,200	115,584	46,233	34,736

5	86,400	8,925	51,945	87,176	234,446	128,200	106,246	42,498	29,027
6	43,200	8,925	46,748	87,176	186,049	128,200	57,849	23,139	14,368
7		8,925	44,288	87,176	140,389	128,200	12,189	4,875	2,752
8		4,461	44,288	87,176	135,925	128,200	7,725	3,090	1,586
9			44,288	87,176	131,464	128,200	3,264	1,305	609
10			44,288	87,176	131,464	128,200	3,264	1,305	554
11			44,288	87,176	131,464	128,200	3,264	1,305	503
12			44,288	87,176	131,464	128,200	3,264	1,305	458
13			44,288	87,176	131,464	128,200	3,264	1,305	416
14			44,288	87,176	131,464	128,200	3,264	1,305	378
15			44,288	87,176	131,464	128,200	3,264	1,305	344
16			22,133	87,176	109,309	128,200	(18,892)	(7,557)	(1,809)
17				87,176	87,176	128,200	(41,024)	(16,410)	(3,571)
37				87,210	87,210	128,250	(41,040)	(16,416)	(531)
38				87,176	87,176	128,200	(41,024)	(16,410)	(483)
39				87,210	87,210	128,250	(41,040)	(16,416)	(439)
40				43,588	43,588	64,100	(20,512)	(8,205)	(199)
Total	750,000	100,000	750,000	3,400,000	5,000,000	5,000,000	0	0	289,526

Note: Years 18–36 have been intentionally omitted.

173

The detailed knowledge of exactly what constitutes say five-year property, and the ability to determine the current cost of each item, is the professional knowledge that is required. We explicitly recommend that a cost seg study be performed by specialists in the field; this is *not* a fertile field for a "do-it-yourself" undertaking. The reason is simple. The IRS will challenge a study that contains mistakes made by people not intimately familiar with the court cases and regulations; the IRS does accept, often without question, a study prepared by a professional whose work they have looked at in the past and approved.

Getting back to Exhibit 14.1, it shows that the analyst has identified some $750,000 of 5-year property, $100,000 of 7-year property, and another $750,000 of 15-year property. The balance of the total cost, kept as 39-year property in this example, is $3,400,000.

Going to row 1, Exhibit 14.1 shows the depreciation expense allowed for each category for year 1, out of the total 39-year expected life for the total. Because of the half-year convention the first year has lower depreciation than years 2 through 39 with another half year in year 40.

Consequently, under this cost seg study the company could in year 1 deduct $245,374 of depreciation, rather than the $64,100 allowed under the normal life schedule of the IRS. This $181,274 of extra depreciation in year 1 is followed in years 2 through 15 with the amounts shown in the "Change in Depreciation Expense" column.

Then in year 16 the depreciation "turns around" and less is allowed for taxes than is permitted for books. This turn around reflects the impact of the shorter lives and accelerated depreciation allowance that has now run its course. This example, of course, is constructed on the assumption that the company does not adopt component depreciation for financial reporting.

Looking at the bottom line of Exhibit 14.1, one sees that on an undiscounted basis there is the same total $5 million of depreciation. Obviously, you are not permitted to charge more total depreciation expense than you paid for the building in the first place.

But because of the time value of money, in this example 10%, the larger expenses allowed in the early year do offset on a present value basis the smaller allowances in subsequent years. In this case there is a net benefit to the taxpayer of $289,526 for the total project life of 39 years. At its peak in the first six years there is an even greater cash-flow benefit but this is partially offset by the turnaround in years 16 through 40. Of course 10% discount rate amounts in years 16 through 39 are worth much less than amounts in year 1 through 16, hence the net savings.

Every time a building is bought by a new owner, that new owner is permitted to perform his own cost seg study on his actual purchase price. This means that if the reader's company has bought a used building it is still permitted to apply a cost seg approach to its purchase price not including land.

The potential cash flow benefits differ for different types of buildings, as a percent of the total cost. Once again, we must caution readers that you cannot take a percent from this schedule and simply claim greater depreciation expense for the early years. Every building has different cost and engineering characteristics and "rules of thumb" no matter how accurate, will not be accepted by the IRS.

A specific report for your building by a cost seg analyst can be prepared that will estimate accurately the anticipated savings based on your actual facts and circumstances. In almost every case there are potential savings that are quite likely to be derived. It behooves every CFO and controller at least to explore the potential savings with every building their company owns.

Our firm's experience is that almost without exception, the first year's tax savings more than pays the total cost of the cost seg study, which might approximate $10,000 to $15,000. Why more building owners do not avail themselves of this tax-saving strategy is one of life's mysteries.

It is our understanding, although you should check with your own tax professional that a cost seg study can be performed in years subsequent to the original purchase. A form is filed with the IRS requesting a "change in accounting." Approval of this request is virtually certain because of prior decisions by tax court. With that approval, it is then possible to file amended corporate returns and obtain a current cash refund for the excess taxes paid, based on the new analysis showing shorter tax lives.

INTERNAL REVENUE SERVICE REVIEW OF A COST SEGREGATION STUDY

For a number of years the IRS seemingly paid little attention to component depreciation developed as a result of cost seg studies. But it was too good to be true for long. As more and more taxpayers had the work performed the reductions in taxes paid became significant. Finally, the IRS fought back.

There have been a number of tax court cases dealing with component depreciation. Some were won by the IRS and others by the taxpayers. But each court decision, on a specific asset classification, has been incorporated into the work of cost seg professionals.

The IRS now has at least four engineering agents who specialize in reviewing cost seg studies. The IRS has developed a detailed audit guide for cost segregation that is to be used by regular revenue agents, not just engineering agents. In the Appendix to this chapter we show a small excerpt of the IRS audit guide. The full text is accessible in the www.IRS.gov web site if you put "cost segregation" in the search box.

It is not necessary for a reader to go through the entire audit guide. It is worthwhile to note that the IRS is starting to take cost seg seriously and is challenging taxpayers' claims if they are not based on sound and approved methodology. We cannot recommend a specific professional organization but as with any professional service there can be variations in fee and professionalism. As a ballpark estimate, however, a cost seg study for a moderate-sized building would cost in the range of $10,000. This amount would be offset through tax savings in well less than a year, with subsequent annual savings falling directly to the bottom line.

This audit guide would help a tax professional who is considering having a cost seg study performed by one of the firms that specialize in this service. Reviewing it would give one an idea of the activities that must be performed and how the IRS reviews it. Inasmuch as cost seg studies in this country are solely for tax purposes it really is up to the company's tax advisors, and the cost seg specialist, to make sure that the work conforms to IRS requirements.

We reiterate again our advice. Other than to have the cost seg work performed in the first place, this is *not* a suitable topic for a Do-It-Yourself approach. While it sounds simple on the surface to break out the costs of the relative components, in practice there are a lot of grey areas that the specialist understands and has had experience in how to handle.

 ## COST SEGREGATION STUDY FOR NEW CONSTRUCTION

Cost segregation studies should be initiated as early in the construction or acquisition process as possible to obtain maximum savings. Consider these three points:

1. If allowed ten minutes with the architect before the design of a building begins, a cost segregation professional can show the architect how to make a larger percentage of the building's components qualify for short-term depreciation thereby increasing the tax savings to the building owner.

2. Special-order building components such as granite counter tops on a reception desk, chandeliers, window coverings, and so on, usually have a higher invoiced cost than can be substantiated from cost estimating guides. There must be proof of these costs in order to report the higher value to the IRS. If granted access to the construction chief before the project breaks ground, a cost segregation specialist will request that five to ten items' costs be set aside for separate reporting. It is often more difficult to track down cost documents further along in the construction process.

3. If a cost segregation study can be performed before the acquisition of a building, personal property can be separated from the building costs. The two costs can then be broken out in the sales agreement and the real property transfer tax basis can be reduced.

The final tax savings may well be the same, but the effort to obtain the information, and hence the cost, will be reduced in terms of the cost seg study.

In some localities there is a property transfer tax. There are potential savings on such property transfer taxes if one separates out personal property from real property, but this is possible only if the analysis is completed *prior* to the closing so the appropriate amounts can be filed on a timely basis. The same analysis, which will help reduce transfer taxes will also be used in the cost seg study, so this really gives great incentive for buyers of real estate to build this directly into the internal procedures and reviews for real estate acquisitions.

 ## WILL COST SEGREGATION LOWER MY PROPERTY TAX EXPENSES?

For assets already owned, do not try and "kill two birds with one stone" by using the cost seg report to try and lower property taxes. They are two separate processes and the property tax aspects are covered in Chapter 11. The quotation below from the Griffin web site pretty much sums up the issues:

"Almost never and be very wary of those who say it does. The rules of real vs. personal property and taxable vs. exempt vary from state to state.

If someone tells you it [cost segregation study] will lower your real and/or personal property taxes—make sure they will be covering the cost of appeals on the assessed valuations if the report is provided to the local assessors.

While performing a cost segregation analysis we have the expertise to check the local property tax assessments and ensure the property is placed on the assessors' tax rolls properly and fairly. If the assessment is found to be inaccurate, we can appeal the assessments to ensure the property is taxed fairly and accurately.

Most often individual states do not follow the same rules as federal income tax on what is real estate vs. personal property; therefore, a cost segregation analysis should **never** be provided to an assessor for use on local property tax assessment purposes. It is simply not apples and apples."[1]

COMPONENTIZATION FOR FINANCIAL REPORTING

There is nothing in GAAP today to preclude U.S. companies from using componentization. But unless there are going to be significant cost savings, which derive on the tax side, the required work effort is diametrically opposite what we recommend overall, and that is not to capitalize small-dollar items. Componentization either has to be done for a total building or it should not be performed at all. You cannot really pick and choose and say, "Well, I'll carve out the HVAC costs for the computer clean room and assign it a five- or- seven year life and leave all the rest of the cost of the building at 39 years."

There are two types of companies in the United States that can effectively use componentization in financial reporting: utilities and defense contractors. Utilities are regulated and their rates are a function of their cost base, so the more they can assign to such assets, the greater will be their allowed return. Besides utilities, defense contractors usually have extraordinarily good property records. This of course is because such contractors are closely audited by the defense contract audit agency and some revenues are in turn based on allowable costs, including depreciation for assets used for the specific contract. If you have a cost-based contract it behooves you to have as many directly assignable costs as you can, and component depreciation is a good way of allocating costs to contracts.

There is one more factor that should be considered, and that is subsequent maintenance. If you have a single large dollar asset on the books, then subsequent smaller expenditures are likely to be considered maintenance and charged to expense. To the contrary, if you have relatively small individual items on the property record, and replace one of them, you will write off the undepreciated cost of the old asset and capitalize the cost of the new replacement.

This tension between expense and capitalization is inherent if a company goes to componentization. In effect a greater amount of subsequent expenditures will be capitalized if each individual component is separately identified. If the entire building is a single line item, then it is almost mandatory to charge almost all subsequent expenditures to expense and you would be precluded from capitalizing them. We are not recommending one way or the other, but readers should be aware of the consequences of either approach.

 ## SUMMARY

While component depreciation is not required for GAAP, as it is for IFRS, there may be some very valid reasons for U.S. companies to consider it. The tax savings alone will easily pay for any cost seg study. If the company then chooses to use the same depreciation expense for financial reporting as for the federal tax return, two things will happen.

First, reported depreciation expense will be higher, although this does not affect cash flow or EBITDA. More rapid depreciation is considered by some analysts to be a "plus." Value line, for example, in their weekly company analyses calculates an overall depreciation rate, with the implication that the faster a company depreciates its assets the better off it is.

The second impact of using cost seg tax lives and depreciation for financial reporting is the elimination of deferred tax assets and liabilities for this category.

Finally, while it is too early to predict whether, or when, IFRS will be used in the United States, Controllers should be fully aware that IFRS not only permits, but requires, componentization. We believe this is the wave of the future, and because of the immediate tax savings, companies would be well advised to start now.

 ## NOTE

1. Griffin Valuation Group web site, Frequently Asked Questions, FAQ, www. griffinvaluation.com

Excerpt of Internal Revenue Service Cost Segregation Audit Guide

S HOWN HERE IS A *small* section from the Internal Revenue Service's (IRS's) Audit Guide on Cost Segregation.

 INTRODUCTION

Cost segregation studies are conducted for a variety of reasons (e.g., income tax, financial accounting, insurance purposes, property tax). For income tax purposes, a cost segregation study involves the allocation (or reallocation) of the total cost (or value) of property into the appropriate property classes in order to compute depreciation deductions. The results of a study are typically summarized in an accompanying report, although there is no standard format for either the study or the report.

The methodology utilized in allocating total project costs to various assets is critical to achieving an accurate cost segregation study. Some of the more common methodologies, and their potential drawbacks, are summarized in this chapter. This discussion should assist the examiner in evaluating the accuracy of a particular study and in performing a risk analysis with respect to the depreciation deductions based on that study.

WHAT ARE THE MOST COMMON METHODOLOGIES UTILIZED FOR COST SEGREGATION STUDIES?

Various methodologies are utilized in preparing cost segregation studies, including the following six:

1. Detailed Engineering Approach from Actual Cost Records
2. Detailed Engineering Cost Estimate Approach
3. Survey or Letter Approach
4. Residual Estimation Approach
5. Sampling or Modeling Approach
6. "Rule of Thumb" Approach

Examiners should not necessarily expect to see these terms mentioned in a study or in a report. Methodologies will also be described in varying detail in different reports. However, based on the information in this chapter, an examiner should be able to recognize the attributes of a given study and identify the methods or approaches used (and also identify the potential drawbacks). It should also be noted that other methodologies may be used, although most are merely derivatives of those enumerated above.

WHAT ARE THE ATTRIBUTES OF VARIOUS COST SEGREGATION METHODOLOGIES?

The following discussion takes a closer look at the main components and attributes of each of the methodologies listed above. Keep in mind that these are the steps normally taken in the preparation of a cost segregation study. The examiner's responsibility is to review the steps taken and evaluate the accuracy of the study, as will be discussed in Chapter 5, "Review and Examination of Cost Segregation Studies."

DETAILED ENGINEERING APPROACH FROM ACTUAL COST RECORDS

The detailed engineering approach from actual cost records, or "detailed cost approach," uses costs from contemporaneous construction and accounting records. In general, it is the most methodical and accurate approach, relying on solid documentation and minimal estimation. Construction-based documentation, such as blueprints, specifications, contracts, job reports, change orders, payment requests, and invoices, are used to determine unit costs. The use of actual cost records contributes to the overall accuracy of cost allocations, although issues may still arise as to the classification of specific assets.

This approach is generally applied only to new construction, where detailed cost records are available. For used or acquired property and for new projects where original construction documents are not available, an alternative approach (e.g., the "detailed engineering cost estimate approach") may be more appropriate.

The detailed cost approach typically includes the following ten activities:

1. Identify the specific project/assets that will be analyzed.
2. Obtain a complete listing of all project costs and substantiate the total project costs.
3. Inspect the facility to determine the nature of the project and its intended use.
4. Photograph specific property items for reference. Request previous site photographs that illustrate the construction progress as well as the condition of the property before the project began.
5. Review "as-built" blueprints, specifications, contracts, bid documents, contractor pay requests, and other construction documentation.
6. Identify and assign specific project items to property classes (e.g., land, land improvements, building, equipment, furniture and fixtures, and other items of tangible personal property).
7. Prepare quantitative "take-offs" for all materials and use payment records to compute unit costs.
8. Apply unit costs to each project component to determine its total cost. Reconcile total costs obtained from quantitative take-offs to total actual costs.
9. Allocate indirect costs, such as architectural fees, engineering fees, and permits, to appropriate assets.
10. Group project items with similar class lives and placed-in-service dates to compute depreciation.

The detailed cost approach is the most time-consuming method and generally provides the most accurate cost allocations. However, the examiner should recognize that the proper classification and costs of § 1245 property could still be an issue with this method.

About the Author

NOW VICE CHAIRMAN OF Marshall & Stevens, **Alfred M. King, CMA, CFM**, was previously Chairman of Valuation Research Corporation, another major international professional firm.

Mr. King's areas of expertise include litigation support, valuation of intangible and intellectual assets, and business valuations. He has been admitted as an expert witness in cases involving damages and business enterprise values. Engagements have been defended before the Internal Revenue Service and before various federal and state courts, including the Southern District of New York, as well as arbitration panels under Federal Guidelines. *In his career to date he has personally valued over $100 Billion of assets.*

Mr. King was Managing Director of the Institute of Management Accountants for ten years where he was responsible for the association's professional activities, including education and research, and for its monthly magazine, *Strategic Finance*. He has spoken widely on a variety of accounting and valuation issues for all the major professional organizations in his field.

A specialist in cost management systems, he has lectured on the subject and has consulted with profit and not-for-profit organizations, as well as several federal government departments. He has taught classes in cost management, accounting, and finance at Fordham University's Graduate School of Business Administration, at the University of Wisconsin—Parkside and at the University of Mary Washington. As a member of the Institute of Management Accounting, and the Financial Executives International, Mr. King has testified extensively before the Securities and Exchange Commission (SEC) and Financial Accounting Standards Board (FASB). Mr. King is a current member of the American Institute of Certified Public Accountants (AICPA) Task Force on Impairment.

Mr. King has written more than 100 articles for professional journals; nine of those that appeared in *Strategic Finance* received certificates of merit as well as a gold, silver, and a bronze medal. In addition, he is the author of two books on cash management, plus *Valuation: What Assets are Really Worth*, published in 2002 by Wiley, *Fair Value for Financial Reporting* published in 2006, and *Executive's Guide to Fair Value* published in 2008. In 2009 he received a certificate for excellence in teaching from the National Association of Certified Valuation Analysts (NACVA).

Mr. King graduated *magna cum laude* in economics from Harvard College in 1954. In 1959, he received an MBA in finance from Harvard Business School. He holds one of the earliest awarded Certificate of Management Accounting, awarded for distinguished performance on the first examination for accreditation. He is listed in the current edition of *Who's Who in America* and *Who's Who in the World.*

Index